PENGUIN BOOKS

Edward IV

A. J. Pollard is a British medieval historian, specializing in the fifteenth century and in particular the Wars of the Roses. A leading authority in the field, he is profesor emeritus of Teesside University. His books include *North-Eastern England during the Wars of the Roses*, *Richard III and the Princes in the Tower*, *Imagining Robin Hood: The Late Medieval Stories in Historical Context* and *Warwick the Kingmaker: Politics, Power and Fame*.

A. J. POLLARD

Edward IV

The Summer King

PENGUIN BOOKS

PENGUIN BOOKS

UK | USA | Canada | Ireland | Australia
India | New Zealand | South Africa

Penguin Books is part of the Penguin Random House group of companies
whose addresses can be found at global.penguinrandomhouse.com.

First published by Allen Lane 2016
First published in Penguin Books 2019
001

Copyright © A. J. Pollard, 2016

The moral right of the author has been asserted

Set in 9.5/13.5 pt Sabon LT Std
Typeset by Jouve (UK), Milton Keynes
Printed and bound in Great Britain by Clays Ltd, Elcograf S.p.A.

ISBN: 978-0-141-98990-7

www.greenpenguin.co.uk

MIX
Paper from
responsible sources
FSC® C018179

Penguin Random House is committed to a
sustainable future for our business, our readers
and our planet. This book is made from Forest
Stewardship Council® certified paper.

Contents

For Scarlett

Preface

Edward IV was a usurper. In 1461, aged eighteen, he seized the throne from Henry VI during the course of the first and most fierce of the Wars of the Roses between his house and the house of Lancaster. His father, Richard, Duke of York, had claimed to be the legitimate king; Edward made good the claim with the sword. Edward struggled at first to hold on to power and was deposed in 1470. Six months later, in the spring of 1471, he dramatically recovered his crown. Uniquely among English monarchs, Edward IV had two reigns. After 1471 he appeared to have secured the throne for himself and his heirs. However, his early death in 1483 led rapidly to the collapse of his dynasty and its replacement by the Tudors. There have been few more dramatic stories in the history of the English monarchy than the rise and fall of the house of York.

Historians are divided as to whether Edward himself is to be blamed for the ultimate failure of his dynasty. Almost from the moment of his death alternative views were being expressed for and against him. Within twenty years a debate concerning the character of the man and the quality of his rule was established with which all subsequent historians have had to engage. This debate, set out in the first chapter, has not been as passionate as that surrounding his brother Richard, Duke of Gloucester, later Richard III, but it has likewise shaped and constrained the way his history is written. Modern judgements of him have ranged from an immoral hedonist and bloody tyrant to a hardworking exemplar of the ideal of a medieval monarch. Within this spectrum, he is in this book characterized nearer the former than the latter, as a ruler who rarely looked beyond the short term, his own close circle and his own immediate ends. Though capable of sustained attention to statecraft, especially in a crisis, as his reign progressed and he aged he became more addicted to self-indulgence. In several respects he was successful, but he failed to establish his dynasty. Yet ill-fortune also played a part. Had he lived for just four more years (he was not yet forty-one when he died in 1483), his elder son would have succeeded him without challenge. It is likely that Edward would then have been remembered as a successful monarch, possibly the founder of a great dynasty. As it is, today he hardly registers in the public imagination, overshadowed by his notorious brother Richard who took the throne for himself.

Edward deserves to be better known – for the drama of his life, his flamboyant personality and the way in which his reign witnessed a revival in royal authority completed by Henry VIII. I hope this brief account will bring him to a wider readership. I would like to thank Tom Penn for asking me to write the book. I have written several times in different contexts on the reign of Edward IV, but never before have I had the opportunity to make the man and monarch centre-stage. I have benefited over a lifetime from the research, assistance and advice of many fellow histori-ans, too many to list, but I would particularly like to acknowledge my debt in this work to Charles Ross and Michael Hicks. I would also like to thank Tig Lang, Hugh Meller and Michael Stansfield for their help on particular matters and all the staff at Penguin in going to press. Finally, Sandra, thank you for your loving support during a difficult time while this book was being written.

The spelling of Middle English has been modernized in all quotations in the text.

Eryholme, December 2015

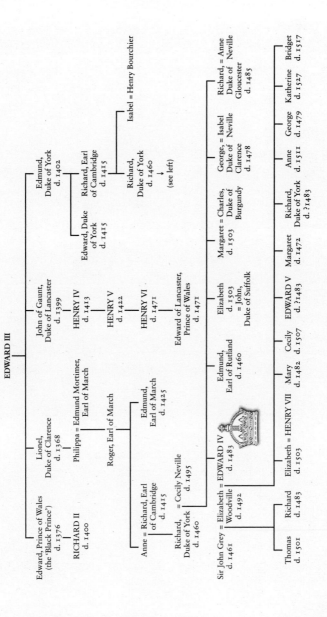

EDWARD III

Edward, Prince of Wales (the 'Black Prince') d. 1376

RICHARD II d. 1400

Lionel, Duke of Clarence d. 1368

Philippa = Edmund Mortimer, Earl of March

Roger, Earl of March

Edmund, Earl of March d. 1425

Anne = Richard, Earl of Cambridge d. 1415

Richard, Duke of York d. 1460 = Cecily Neville d. 1495

John of Gaunt, Duke of Lancaster d. 1399

HENRY IV d. 1413

HENRY V d. 1422

HENRY VI d. 1471

Edward of Lancaster, Prince of Wales d. 1471

Edmund, Duke of York d. 1402

Richard, Earl of Cambridge d. 1415

Edward, Duke of York d. 1415

Richard, Duke of York d. 1460 → (see left)

Isabel = Henry Bourchier

Sir John Grey = Elizabeth Woodville d. 1461 d. 1492

Thomas d. 1501

Richard d. 1483

Elizabeth = EDWARD IV d. 1483 d. 1483

Elizabeth = HENRY VII d. 1503

Mary d. 1482

Cecily d. 1507

Edmund, Earl of Rutland d. 1460

EDWARD V d. ?1483

Margaret d. 1472

Richard, Duke of York d. ?1483

Margaret = Charles, Duke of Burgundy d. 1503

Elizabeth d. 1503 = John, Duke of Suffolk

George, = Isabel Duke of Neville Clarence d. 1478

Anne d. 1511

George d. 1479

Richard, = Anne of Neville Duke of Gloucester d. 1485

Katherine d. 1527

Bridget d. 1517

Edward IV

I
A Notable Foundation of Hearsay

Many people know that the winter of discontent was made glorious summer by the sun of York. Not so many are aware that the opening lines of Shakespeare's *Richard III* celebrate the resumption of the reign of Edward IV of York. Edward had been deposed in October 1470 and his predecessor, the Lancastrian Henry VI, restored. By one of the most remarkable reverses of fortune in English history, he recovered his throne six months later. Shakespeare starts the action at this moment of triumph in the spring of 1471, when the son of Richard of York, who used the sun as one of his badges, began his second reign.

Shakespeare did not devote a play in his history cycle to Edward IV, choosing to split his reign between *Henry VI, Part 3* and *Richard III*. His decision to some extent reflected a Tudor perception that Henry VI was the legitimate king until 1471, but also followed from his instinct that Richard III was a far more dramatic subject. In *Henry VI* Edward is a cruel, dishonest and duplicitous usurper, overshadowed by an heroic Warwick the Kingmaker. In *Richard III* he is a bit player upon the stage, now a sick and pliable king, largely irrelevant to the course of events being manipulated by his Machiavellian brother. This is a travesty. For it was only after 1471 that Edward was able to enjoy his hard-won crown and to rule much as he pleased. Assessment of Edward IV as a monarch largely depends on these later years. When he died in 1483 there seemed to be no threat to the peaceful succession of his son, another Edward, to the throne.

The opening lines of *Richard III* also echo the fact that the twelve years of Edward's second reign came to be regarded as a short-lived golden age of 'glorious summer', before winter descended once again as a result of his brother Richard's usurpation. One consequence is that these years can appear to be but a brief respite in the apparently relentless chaos of the Wars of the Roses that stretched from 1455 to beyond 1485. Because of this, as well as Shakespeare's dramatic licence, Edward IV has tended to be a little-known king, dismissed in many traditional accounts as of only passing interest. This has been reinforced by the image of the monarch as a shallow playboy who preferred, in Shakespeare's words, to caper 'nimbly in a lady's chamber' to the 'lascivious pleasing of a lute' than to attend to the serious business of war and government.

Contemporaries and near-contemporaries were more positive. Two narratives in particular have endured: one by a cleric, a middle-ranking civil servant and member of Edward's household who wrote the anonymous memoir for Crowland Abbey, the Lincolnshire monastery from which it took its name; the other by the Flemish courtier and diplomat Philippe de Commynes. Both were contemporaries of Edward and both had met him and were eyewitnesses to some events. Both set down their memoirs after Edward's death – indeed, after the accession of Henry VII and the failure of the Yorkist dynasty. Thus, though written by contemporaries, they were composed with the benefit of hindsight and under later influences.

The Crowland author was an admirer of his 'illustrious' king, though not uncritical. He was somewhat in awe of him, praising him as a magnificent monarch, prudent and far-seeing, in full command of his kingdom in his later years. But he disapproved of his dissipated lifestyle, his financial exactions and his tyrannical tendencies at the end of his reign. Although some of this author's judgements have been found wanting in the light of other evidence, he remains the best-informed, the fullest and most reliable source for the reign.[1]

Commynes first served the Duke of Burgundy, the ruler of Flanders and the rest of the Low Countries, before transferring his loyalty, contentiously, to Burgundy's rival and overlord, King Louis XI of France, in 1472. He never visited England though was in Calais, the remaining English possession in France, on several occasions, and received news and information from English diplomats, exiles and merchants. Commynes offered contradictory assessments of Edward. At one point in his memoirs he commented that he was not an outstanding man and at another he reported that Warwick considered him a little simple ('a bit thick'?). Yet he also states that he was a very great and powerful king, fearing nobody after 1471. On one thing he was consistent: Edward was not to be compared in statecraft with his own king, Louis XI. A strikingly handsome man in his youth, Edward was more concerned with the pursuit of pleasure than the art of ruling and was more prone to random acts of cruelty than Louis.[2]

The two portraits are not far apart. On one matter both authors are in full-hearted agreement: Edward's prowess on the field of battle and his outstanding success as a general. The crucial differences derive from their affiliation. They both admired the masters they had served and considered them distinguished monarchs. Thus Crowland saw Edward as one of the more successful English kings; Commynes considered him naïve and no match for the cunning Louis.

Several of the faults that Crowland and Commynes perceived in Edward are to be found also in the account given by Dominic Mancini, an Italian visitor resident in London in the summer of 1483, of how Richard III became king. It was composed before the end of that year, but lost until the twentieth century. It contains a pen portrait of Edward in his last months, drawing heavily on what was being said in London that summer; it repeats the view that, while affable, he was excessive in his womanizing, avaricious and too much in the grip of a faction.[3] These criticisms derived from the charges against Edward's regime made by Richard III at the time.

Richard III's denigration of his brother to justify his usurpation of the throne in 1483 may also have influenced the memoirs written later by Crowland and Commynes. It is, of course, difficult to discern whether Richard III's accusations were well founded or not: clever propagandists base their accounts on a modicum of truth. Because of this even the most immediate and apparently reliable of our narrative sources, which have shaped the way we see Edward IV, are problematic.

The first historians who wrote about Edward IV in the reign of Henry VIII, Polydore Vergil and Sir Thomas More, still in touch with contemporary memories, tended to confirm the view of Crowland. Vergil considered that Edward was an effective monarch, diligent as a ruler, affable, but regrettably avaricious and given over to bodily lust.[4] Sir Thomas More's portrait in his history of Richard III carries a panegyric of Edward who, despite his self-indulgence and 'fleshly wantonness', was courageous, just, merciful and wise, loved by his subjects, and ruled benignly over a peaceful and prosperous kingdom. Yet elsewhere in the work, in the mouth of Richard III's ally the Duke of Buckingham, More reiterates criticism of the king for his avarice, his sexual excesses and his failure to control faction.[5]

There are other contemporary or near-contemporary sources, unearthed in subsequent centuries, that can flesh out the history. There are several narratives, chronicles and related accounts, such as versions of the London Chronicles and the chronicle known as the Brut, completed or continued in the 1460s, which are valuable for the events of 1459–61, though they reflect the Yorkist version.[6] Two narratives composed in or after 1470–71 give a version of events from the victorious side.[7] The main independent account is that written in about 1480 by John Warkworth which takes the narrative up to 1473.[8]

Also invaluable for details are diplomatic correspondence, private letters, aristocratic, urban and ecclesiastical archives and, above all, the public records of government. All these have been exploited intensively, especially in the last century, to amplify and deepen our knowledge and understanding of Edward IV and his reign.[9] Yet collectively they have not affected significantly the overarching interpretations of the reign inherited from the first memoirs and histories. Sir Philip Sidney's scathing judgement of the historian 'loaden with old mouse-eaten records, authorising himself (for the most part) upon other histories, whose greatest authorities are built upon the notable foundation of hearsay' is not far off the mark.[10]

In Sidney's time, the late sixteenth century, the positive evaluation of Edward IV waned. A view developed that Edward was an immoral, cruel and deceitful king solely driven by lust, avarice and casual cruelty (as reflected in Shakespeare).[11] By the mid nineteenth century he came to be represented as a despot, more vicious than any king since John and more cruel and bloodthirsty, whose rule was unconstitutional and arbitrary.[12] Edward IV was cast as a hinderer of democracy, a reactionary, laying the foundation for the absolute rule of Tudor despotism. A school textbook first published in 1909 summed him up: 'He was one of the worst men who ever sat on the throne of England and his premature end was due to his evil living.'[13]

In the twentieth century some historians began once again to take a more positive view. Edward has now been praised as one of the greatest of English kings, a man who rescued his kingdom from a 'shambles' and left his dynasty secure on the throne; a king who came close to perfecting the medieval system of personal monarchy.[14] However, not all are as impressed. On the contrary, 'this heavy eating, heavy drinking and heavy whoring king' lacked judgement, was complacent and largely ineffective as a monarch, failing to reunite his kingdom after civil war and allowing faction to flourish with disastrous results after his premature death.[15] To some he was hard-working; possessed of 'profound political ability', of 'iron will and great fixity of purpose' beneath a shroud of 'indolence and gaiety'; to others he was no more than the shroud itself: an 'indolent, sensual and selfish hedonist'.[16] As the number of works published about the later fifteenth century and Edward IV has expanded rapidly, especially in the last thirty years, so have all manner of variations between these different positions proliferated. However, all remain within the framework created in the last two decades of the fifteenth century, and are variations on the themes established then about the man and the monarch. Any modern life of Edward IV and history of his reign is inevitably both shaped and constrained by this tradition.

2
Son of York

Edward IV was born in Rouen on 28 April 1442, the second but eldest surviving son of Richard Plantagenet, Duke of York and his duchess Cecily, née Neville. Edward's birth in Normandy, where his father was serving as the king's Lieutenant-General and Governor towards the end of the Hundred Years War, would later give rise to rumours of illegitimacy. Such slurs about royal princes born abroad were not uncommon. Commynes picked it up: he even named the Rouen archer who was supposedly the father.[1] However, there is no unequivocal or substantial evidence to support the notion that Edward IV was conceived in adultery.[2] Rumours of his mother's infidelity first emerged in the late 1460s, in the latter part of Edward's first abortive reign, and would resurface after his death, when his youngest brother Richard, Duke of Gloucester seized the throne for himself. During this troubled time it was being said that, in her fury at Edward's marriage to the arriviste Elizabeth Woodville in 1464, his mother 'fell into such a frenzy that she asserted that he was not the offspring of her husband but conceived in adultery'.[3] In the days leading up to his usurpation of the throne Richard III was reported to have claimed first that Edward, who 'in every way was unlike his father', was illegitimate, but had then back-tracked, arguing that it was Edward's sons – the princes who would disappear inside the Tower – who were bastards, not their father.[4] In Richard's official declaration of his title to the throne, passed as an act of parliament several months later, this claim recurs as a not very subtle aside that Richard III was certainly his father's son:

> we consider how you are the undoubted son and heir of Richard, late duke of York, very inheritor of the said crown and dignity royal ... and how you were born within this land.[5]

Edward was a royal prince, descended directly from Edward III. During the late 1450s his father, Richard of York, came to believe that he was the legitimate king of England denied his royal dignity by the usurping house of Lancaster, though it is not certain that he already held this belief at the time of Edward's birth. Back in 1400 Richard II, the grandson of the great Plantagenet king Edward III, died childless. He had already been deposed by the first Lancastrian king, Henry IV, who traced his own royal descent through his father, John of Gaunt, Duke of Lancaster, Edward III's third son. But Edward III's second and fourth sons (his first, the Black Prince, was long dead) also had legitimate issue, lines of descent that, in 1411, combined together to produce Richard of York. Richard inherited the duchy at the age of four after both his father and uncle, who was childless, died in 1415. Edward IV was therefore born the heir of a great magnate and had inherited the patrimonies of two of Edward III's sons. As the descendant of Edward III's second son Lionel, Duke of Clarence, albeit through the female line – Clarence's daughter and granddaughter – Edward's father also had a claim, controversially based on the superiority of the female line, to be the true and legitimate inheritor of the crown of England.

When he was three, the young Edward was acknowledged as Earl of March, the title of his great-uncle, the last of the notable Welsh Marcher family of Mortimer.[6] He enjoyed a conventional upbringing for one of his high birth, first in his mother's household, possibly much of the time at the family seat of Fotheringhay Castle in Northamptonshire, where his younger brother Richard was born in 1452. From the age of seven, as was customary, separate provision was made for his residence and education in courtesy, letters and the martial arts at Ludlow Castle, the principal seat of the Mortimer family. A letter of 1454 from Edward and his younger brother Edmund to their father has survived in which they assured him that they were attending to their learning, but complained also of the behaviour of two fellow pupils in this little aristocratic school.[7] Although royal blood flowed through his veins, Edward was educated conventionally as a nobleman, not as a king-in-waiting.

England was in crisis during Edward IV's adolescence. The king, Henry VI, was ineffectual; he was fundamentally uninterested in governing, leaving almost all of it to his ministers and courtiers. Moreover, in 1453 his mental health collapsed and although he recovered at the end of

1454, it remained fragile thereafter. He had presided over the loss not only of his father Henry V's conquests in France but also in 1453 the duchy of Gascony, which had been held by England for 300 years. The long struggle to retain the French possessions had bankrupted the crown. Moreover, deep recession from the 1440s onwards had further impoverished the realm. In 1450 a popular uprising, known as Cade's Revolt, swept through south-eastern England. As the government of Henry VI floundered so lawlessness increased, especially among the landed classes, whose feuds were allowed to fester. Not surprisingly, the higher nobility, who had done their best to hold the kingdom together during Henry VI's long minority, became divided between those in power and those excluded from it.

Chief among the excluded was Edward's father Richard of York, between 1447 and 1453 the closest living male relation to the king, who pursued a vendetta against Edmund Beaufort, Duke of Somerset who was high in royal favour and whom he blamed for the loss of Henry V's conquests in France. He sought several times, without success, to force himself into government. In 1454, when Henry VI was ill, he was made protector of the realm. At that time he forged an alliance with the powerful Neville family, both Richard, Earl of Salisbury and his more charismatic son, also Richard, Earl of Warwick.

At an early age, as Richard of York's heir and nominal representative in the Marches of Wales, the young Edward began to be associated with his father's political career. In 1452, aged ten, Edward was rumoured to be at the head of a force of Marcher men raised to support his father's armed demonstration against the Lancastrian government. Two years later, in January 1454, he accompanied his father when he rode in strength up to Westminster to press his claim to open a session of parliament on behalf of the incapacitated Henry VI.[8] In neither of these instances could the boy have been acting on his own initiative; clearly he was being groomed as the figurehead of the duke's Marcher interests. Yet later, between 1456 and 1459, when there were several disturbances in the area in which Richard of York's lieutenants were involved, young Edward himself was not implicated. In his early teens, as he was honing his martial skills, he was kept deliberately out of the limelight.

Edward's entry on to the political stage took place, unsurprisingly enough, in the Welsh Marches where he had received his education. But the dramatic nature of his emergence as a political player could not have been foretold.[9] In the late summer of 1459, Edward's father Richard of York and his allies, the Neville Earls of Warwick and Salisbury, once again resorted to arms to try to impose themselves on the Lancastrian government of Henry VI. Salisbury was to bring troops from the north of England, Warwick from his stronghold of Calais; Richard of York, with the seventeen-year-old Edward now at his side, raised the Marches of Wales. The Yorkists may have been planning to rendezvous at Warwick, but they found themselves outmanoeuvred and retreated to Ludlow, where they prepared to make a stand. But the desertion of some of their men led the commanders to abandon their position. On the night of 12 October they fled: Richard of York, with his second son Edmund, Earl of Rutland, made his way to Dublin; Edward, with Salisbury and Warwick, escaped with difficulty via Devon to Calais. Thus began for Edward a passage from childhood to adulthood by the sword that no ritual ceremony could have matched.

The routed Yorkists did not command much support among the lords and gentry, the political nation of the kingdom. They thus appealed to the people as a whole. Simmering unrest had continued in south-eastern England since the suppression of Cade's Revolt in 1450. The roots of discontent lay in the failures of Henry VI's government, especially the loss of France, and the heavy burden of taxation his wars had incurred, exacerbated by recession. This was not the discontent of the downtrodden poor. The commons, as the people as a whole were known, contained many gradations of rank, status and wealth between the vagabond or labourer and the yeoman or merchant. 'The middling sorts' in town and country, men of some independent substance, had a significant stake in the kingdom, as lesser local officers of the crown, manor and Church, as taxpayers, as voters in elections and in many small boroughs as Members of Parliament.[10]

Normal political participation in England in the mid fifteenth century was not restricted to the great landed, ecclesiastical and mercantile elites. It was the same middle-standing countrymen and townsmen, lesser gentlemen, yeomen, more prosperous husbandmen, artisans, shopkeepers and small-scale tradesmen who predominated in protests. When they and the communities they led believed that the crown was failing in its obligation to maintain law and order and to promote the public good, they took to the streets, often in arms, brandishing petitions for the reform of grievances. They bore arms because they also formed the local militia, required to possess weapons and to train regularly for the defence of the realm. Like their betters, they believed that *in extremis* the use of force was politically justified for the greater good. Popular uprisings, no less than aristocratic rebellions, were the extension of politics by other means.

In the late 1450s the Yorkists harnessed popular discontent to their cause. In manifestos issued in 1459 and 1460, recycling the complaints of 1450, they claimed that they were in rebellion against the king in the name of the common good to reform the kingdom. They mobilized the militia in Kent and neighbouring counties, who had risen in 1450, to fight alongside them.

Thus the Yorkist rebellion raised deeper political issues. At a parliament called to Coventry in the autumn of 1459, Henry VI's government proscribed the Yorkists and declared them traitors by the process of attainder (their noble blood having been tainted by treason); their forfeited estates were redistributed to their enemies. The government also countered the Yorkists' claim that they could act in the name of the common good against the crown. No subject, it asserted, had the right to use force against the king, no subject had the right to act independently of the crown. Only the sovereign could ensure that the realm was governed for the common good. The absolute sovereignty of the crown was reasserted, but the existence of the belief in an alternative, popular, source of sovereignty was implicitly acknowledged.

Holed up in Calais for six months, Edward and his Neville kinsmen, the Earls of Warwick and Salisbury, withstood assaults on the city by Lancastrian forces under the Duke of Somerset. In January 1460 one Lancastrian commander, Richard Woodville, Lord Rivers, was captured in a naval raid on the Kentish port of Sandwich together with his son Sir Anthony and taken back to Calais. There, according to one report, they were berated by the Yorkist lords – including Edward – for their pretensions to nobility, which was hardly warranted given their lineage and record of service. Later Edward would change his mind about the Woodvilles; the Earl of Warwick, however, would not.[11]

By June Edward, Warwick and Salisbury were ready to launch an invasion of England. The ground had been prepared that spring by a daring mission to Dublin by the Earl of Warwick, where he consulted with Richard of York, and by the seizure of Sandwich. The invasion, led by Warwick, met little resistance. It became a triumphal progress through Kent, which rose in his favour, and into London, where his stock was high, to Northampton, near which the Yorkists won a comprehensive victory over Henry VI's forces, helped by significant Lancastrian desertions. Ever mindful of popular opinion, Warwick had given the order to spare the commons but kill the opposition leaders. After the battle the unfortunate King Henry VI, now merely a pawn in the game of politics, fell into Yorkist hands. He was taken to London a prisoner; there his government was reconfigured and the royal household purged. From now on Henry VI was to be king in name only and England to be ruled on his behalf by Richard of York and his allies.

York himself did not return to England from Ireland until September. Landing in the north-west, at Chester, he delayed his journey to Westminster to coincide with the opening of parliament called for October. On his progress south he adopted the style of king and on his arrival strode into the Lords' chamber, where he claimed the throne as the true heir of Richard II. He had abandoned the stance of reformer in the name of the common good: he trumped the Lancastrian assertion that royal sovereignty was absolute by claiming that he was the legitimate king. Caught between a reluctance to depose Henry VI, a crowned king of England, and the palpable military threat of the Yorkists, parliament prevaricated. After several weeks a compromise was reached in November by which Henry remained king for his life, but York was adopted as his heir. It was clearly unworkable. Lancastrian loyalists – foremost among them Henry VI's French queen, Margaret of Anjou, who had emerged as a key player in government – would never accept the disinheritance of her son Edward, Prince of Wales. The Yorkists themselves may have been divided. Some reports suggested that the earls were surprised by York's move – something which may well have been true of the older Earl of Salisbury. His son, the Earl of Warwick, may have been party to the plan even though he denied it – he had after all met with Richard of York in Dublin earlier in the year to plan the invasion. Edward, already under Warwick's charismatic influence, presumably accepted – even welcomed – his father's bid for the throne.

First, however, the Yorkists had to assert their authority over the kingdom. The north and Wales remained in their enemies' hands, and Queen Margaret's lieutenants were assembling a large army in Yorkshire. Richard of York himself, probably not fully aware of the strength of her army, marched north to confront her. By Christmas he, his second son Edmund, Earl of Rutland and the Earl of Salisbury managed to reach his Yorkshire castle of Sandal, but no further. Near there, on the penultimate day of the year, they were surprised by a Lancastrian force and overwhelmed. Richard of York and Rutland were killed; Salisbury was captured and promptly executed at the nearby castle of Pontefract.

Meanwhile Edward, as Earl of March, had been despatched to the Welsh Marches, where the careful cultivation of him as heir of the Mortimer family now paid off. There he was able to rally the family's principal retainers and tenants to confront forces under Jasper Tudor, Earl of Pembroke. Now Duke of York following the death of his father, Edward overcame them on 2 February 1461 at Mortimer's Cross, near Wigmore. Shortly after dawn, before battle began, a parhelion, whereby through the atmospheric effect on a cold, bright morning there seem to be three suns, appeared in the eastern sky. Edward took this as a portent of his success, and duly won.[12] Pembroke escaped, but Owen Tudor, his father – and grandfather of the future Henry VII – was captured and executed without trial at Hereford. This was but the first of a series of killings of captured enemies carried out by Edward in the battles that followed. Mortimer's Cross was also the first in Edward's sequence of victories: he commemorated the portent by adopting the sun in splendour as his badge alongside the white rose.[13]

Edward had taken control of the Welsh Marches. However, two weeks later the Earl of Warwick, who had marched out of London to confront the Lancastrian army approaching from the north, was overwhelmed at St Albans. He managed to escape and joined Edward, now moving west, in the Cotswolds. Without hesitation the two noblemen marched on the capital; arriving before Margaret of Anjou, they took control of the city. Although after St Albans Queen Margaret had been reunited with Henry VI and their young son and heir, she had fatally hesitated. Edward and Warwick wasted no time in declaring that the November Act of Accord was null and void and that Edward, by right, was the true king of England. On 4 March Warwick orchestrated an 'election' in which the Yorkist army, made up of county levies 'representing' the people, acclaimed Edward as their king. He assumed the crown. Yorkist propagandists were busy. 'Let us walk in a new vineyard,' ran an exhortatory slogan, 'and let us make us a gay garden in the month of March with this fair white rose and herb, the Earl of March.'[14]

The new king wasted no time in reorganizing and reinforcing his army and setting off in pursuit of the Lancastrian host retreating to its northern base. He caught up with it at the crossing of the River Aire in Yorkshire at Ferrybridge.

In a two-day running battle, culminating near Towton on 29 March, the Lancastrian army was overwhelmed. This was the bloodiest battle of the war, indeed of the Wars of the Roses, in which many Lancastrian lords were killed. Henry VI and Margaret of Anjou fled to Scotland. After mopping-up operations, which took Edward as far north as Newcastle upon Tyne, the victorious new king returned leisurely and in triumph to London.

Edward had revealed a precocious military talent. The victories that had secured the throne were undoubtedly his. While he had experienced men at his side at Towton, including William Neville, Lord Fauconberg, uncle to the Earl of Warwick and a veteran of the Hundred Years War, these battles were won by his leadership and in particular his personal prowess, leading from the front and trading blows in the midst of the mêlée. There was nothing sophisticated about Edward's approach to battle: his remarkably effective strategy was to get at the enemy as soon as possible and immediately engage them head-on. He was a young man who inspired his men by his undoubted courage.

Edward's voice probably carried little weight until after his father's death. But given what he revealed of himself in the first months of 1461, he most likely did not think twice about marching immediately on London in late February or pursuing the retreating Lancastrians as soon as he could. These bold decisions by a raw youth changed the course of the civil war. The more cautious and seasoned Earl of Warwick may well have been carried along by his daring; it was, though, probably a joint decision to seize the throne. Warwick, who was bolder politically than Richard of York had been, may well have argued that this should have been done in the previous autumn; Edward would have agreed with him. But in the event it was the fearless Edward himself, not Warwick, who made good his father's claim and took the throne for the house of York.

3
This Fair White Rose

Edward IV was crowned king on 28 June 1461, at the age of nineteen. His road to the throne had been remarkable. Eighteen months earlier, in the late autumn of 1459, he had not yet entered public life: when he fled to Calais with Warwick, he was barely on the threshold of taking command of his own earldom of March. He had no experience of government or administration. But during the tumultuous one and a half years that brought him to the throne, he had learned quickly about the twists and turns of political fortune and the reality of war.

The victory was the fruit of an alliance between an untested and headstrong novice and a wily and experienced politician. They made a formidable partnership. Contemporaries focused in particular on the role of the Earl of Warwick, who enjoyed a high reputation abroad and was credited with placing Edward on the throne. Warwick, indeed, was generally assumed by foreign observers to be the real power in the kingdom: Commynes later recalled that he governed the king and directed his affairs. A joke did the rounds in France that there were two kings in England, one the Earl of Warwick and another whose name could not be recalled.[1] As many people saw it,

Edward, as he began his reign, was in the shadow of the mighty earl.

It is true that the Earl of Warwick and his connections played a prominent role in helping Edward take the throne and in securing the new regime in the years that followed.[2] This proved difficult: there were Lancastrians at large in Wales and in the north. Warwick and his brother John Neville, newly promoted Lord Montagu, assumed responsibility for the north, but it was to take three years and three attempts finally to secure Northumberland, where Lancastrian resistance was sustained by Scottish and French aid. Warwick was also prominent in diplomacy as the regime sought – successfully – to prevent a grand Franco-Scottish alliance in support of the house of Lancaster. His brother George, Bishop of Exeter was chancellor and oversaw royal administration, as well as being deeply involved in diplomacy. Edward himself dealt with Wales and the Marches, riding up there after his coronation to reassert his authority. He left his own lieutenants, most notably William Herbert of Raglan, to complete the job – something they never quite managed.

The young king threw himself into his new role, dealing personally with matters great and small.[3] He presided over the parliament that met in the autumn of 1461. In the formal statement of his title to the throne, declared in its first session, Edward reiterated his legitimate right to it, condemned Henry VI as the heir of a usurper who had finally forfeited his throne by his failure to accept the November Accord and blamed him for all the 'unrest, inward war and trouble . . . abuse of the laws, riot, extortion, murder, rape and vicious living' that had plagued England in recent years.[4] Edward, or his servants on his behalf, also called upon a long-established body of arcane prophetic literature, set out in elaborately decorated pedigrees, to buttress his claim and represent him as the promised saviour of Britain (Wales). These purported to demonstrate that he was descended through the Mortimers from the ancient Welsh princes and ultimately the legendary kings of Britain who, it had been foretold, would one day rule the land again. In this way he was sometimes represented as wearing three crowns, as King of England, King of France, and King of Britain.[5]

Edward dealt in person with a series of risings in the West Country and the Midlands in the summer of 1462. In the autumn he raised an army to march north, to assist the Earl of Warwick and confront the Scots but, struck down at Durham by measles, or perhaps smallpox, he left it to Warwick to subdue Northumberland for a second time. Then it was back to Westminster for a second session of parliament in April 1463. A new rebellion in Northumberland supported by the Scots led him to declare his intention to invade that country, and enabled him to secure a grant of taxation for the purpose. But, with Edward's attention diverted again by further unrest in central England and the pursuit of a diplomatic solution to the Scottish threat, the invasion never materialized; the Nevilles once again held the line against England's northern neighbour.

Edward and his advisers were also engaged in structuring a new regime. Those who had fought against the king were attainted and their estates confiscated by the crown, much of the plunder being redistributed to reward York-ist supporters. Punishment and revenge were balanced with mercy and reconciliation, not always successfully. Many great families, prominently the Beauforts, Percys, Hollands, Courtenays, Tudors and Cliffords, remained unreconciled to the new regime.[6] In 1462 the execution of the Earl of Oxford, probably for failing to reveal his son and heir Aubrey's treason (Aubrey was executed alongside him), made a lifelong enemy of his second son, John, the new earl. An attempt to end the feud between York and Beaufort, which had remained unabated since 1450, by pardoning and welcoming the new Duke Henry of Somerset to court in 1463 failed humiliatingly when the duke rebelled again.[7] The Yorkists had never represented the majority of the political nation – and, it was clear, still did not. The deposition of Henry VI, who was yet at large, had not won general acceptance. Edward's was a minority regime.

His distribution of rewards was balanced between followers of the houses of Neville and York. The Earl of Warwick himself was allowed a free hand in the north of England, where he ruled almost independently of the king. Many of his men profited, a number of his servants and councillors entered royal service and several sat on the king's council. But from the start the Nevilles did not have it all their own way. Edward endowed and promoted his surviving younger brothers, George aged twelve and Richard, nine, the elder being created Duke of Clarence and the younger Duke of Gloucester. Kinsmen such as Viscount Bourchier, created Earl of Essex, were stalwart in their support; and the king built on and strengthened the following he inherited from his father, prominent among whom were the newly ennobled William, Lord Herbert, William, Lord Hastings and Humphrey Stafford of Southwick, created Earl of Devon. Edward was fortunate in that the civil wars had created thirteen vacancies among the twenty-four Knights of the Garter. He himself was the first new member. He filled many of the remaining stalls with those who had fought for him to win the throne.

Edward declared at the beginning of his reign his determination to tackle lawlessness. The kingdom, one favourable chronicler wrote, had for a long time been out of all good governance.[8] The most important function expected of a king by his subjects was the provision of justice and the maintenance of law and order. Administered by the law courts in Westminster – King's Bench for breaches of the king's peace (criminal law), and Common Pleas for cases between subject and subject, what we now call civil law – it was extended into the provinces through assizes, quarter sessions and, at the lowest level, manorial courts. The supreme law court was parliament, where the law was amended by statute. Enhanced by prerogative courts, such as Chancery (equitable jurisdiction) and the Constable's Court (jurisdiction over treason) and the use of special commissions of oyer and terminer (hear and determine) to deal with major outbreaks of disorder, Edward IV had at his disposal a complex and sophisticated system.[9] He was keen to demonstrate his intention to restore good government, sitting on one occasion in a session of King's Bench.

Edward inherited an established if cumbersome bureaucracy located in Westminster. Routine government, the

day-to-day administration of the realm – such as the issu-
ing of royal grants and administrative orders to sheriffs
and other local officers of the crown, or the collection of
parliamentary taxes, and customs and excise – lay with the
Chancery, Privy Seal and Exchequer.[10] The most ancient
secretarial office, the Chancery, had become highly for-
malized; the Privy Seal, too, which originated as the king's
personal authorization for action, had evolved into an
established office with its own formal routines.

Edward immediately introduced practices derived from
the administration of aristocratic estates with which he
was familiar. He developed the office of his secretary in his
own household as the key agent of his government, often
bypassing the offices of state by use of letters authorized by
his signet, issued directly to his subjects. Similarly the
financial administration of the king's own lands was taken
over by the officers of the King's Chamber (the financial
office of the king's own household), bypassing the unwieldy
Exchequer. While these measures did not at first lead to
any significant overall financial improvement, they did
speed cash flow.

In most matters, the king was advised by his council.
The royal council, the precursor of the Privy Council,
which normally met in Westminster was an informal body
with no fixed constitution or terms of reference. Besides
offering counsel on matters of high policy, it supervised
routine government. It acted from time to time as an equitable court, resolving disputes between subjects. How much
Edward independently determined policy in these years
is impossible to tell. One suspects that of necessity he

followed the advice of his council on many matters. He no doubt initiated those policies that concerned his family or his prerogative, such as rewards and pardons. Because of his inexperience, and perhaps a lack of interest in the detail of government, he may have depended heavily on others in matters of state as well as day-to-day administration.

Parliament was an extended meeting of council, in which the king consulted with his peers in the House of Lords and representatives of the counties and boroughs in the House of Commons. It met only at the king's pleasure. It legislated by statute, but its position was guaranteed by its sole authority to vote taxes on behalf of the king's subjects. The basic form of tax was a levy of one-tenth of the value of the goods of townspeople and one-fifteenth of those of country people. By Edward's reign these had long been fixed as sums due from each community, who raised their contributions according to local custom and practice. The yield from one 'tenth and fifteenth' was in theory £31,000, in practice less.

The crown was bankrupt in 1461. At the beginning of his reign Edward received a regular income, excluding parliamentary tenths and fifteenths, of no more than £50,000 a year, half from customs and excise, tunnage and poundage voted as a matter of course by parliament from meeting to meeting, and half from the king's landed estate, his private income. The equivalent income had been £120,000 in 1399. The collapse in royal revenue was partly the consequence of trade recession in the mid fifteenth century, partly the result of the collapse of the value of land following population decline over the preceding century, but also the crippling cost of outstanding loans to pay for the war in France before 1453 and the financial incompetence of Henry VI himself. There was no immediate end to recession: indeed matters were made worse by a devaluation of the coinage in 1464–5, which, although it brought in an immediate windfall and made English exports cheaper, triggered a trade war with Flanders. Edward did benefit from an increase in the royal estate: the duchy of York and earldom of March were added to it. He also confiscated a significant amount of land from his defeated enemies, but the financial advantage of this was soon nullified by the need to reward his own supporters.

In his first three years Edward needed all his wits to hold the throne. He was the victor in a civil war. He ruled through his own household, very much as the great aristocrat he had been educated to be. He did not turn twenty-one, the age of majority, until April 1463. By 1464, even before Lancastrian resistance in the north had been finally subdued, he began to feel more secure, to take his ease and to enjoy his new prosperity. By all accounts he was a good-looking, strapping youth: well over six feet tall,[11] companionable and charming. He was singularly fitted to be king, so the formal statement of his title to the throne declared in 1461, by the 'beauty of your personage it has pleased Almighty God to send you' as well as his proven 'princely and knightly prowess and courage'. According to the Flemish diplomat and chronicler Philippe de Commynes, Edward was the most handsome prince of his generation.[12] He was well educated and accomplished, spoke French competently and read Latin.[13] He had made a name for himself as a dashing soldier, but he also enjoyed the youthful pursuits of peace. All his life he took every opportunity, as many of his class did, to hunt. When en route supposedly to invade Scotland in August 1463, he stopped at Fotheringhay for the chase. As Lord Hastings wrote to a councillor of the Duke of Burgundy Jean de Lannoy, perhaps with a nudge and a wink, he was 'at his sport and entertainment of the hunt'.[14]

For such weeks of entertainment were also occasions for dalliance. He was a bachelor who in his youth seems to have had a penchant for aristocratic widows. One of his earliest conquests was Elizabeth Lucy, who might already have been a sixteen-year-old widow in 1461, when their relationship may have started.[15] Another, possibly dating from the same year, may have been Eleanor, née Talbot, the widow of Sir Thomas Butler, a few years older than the king.[16] His practice of staying on progress at the houses of other young widows tantalizingly hints at more seductions.[17] It may also have been his habit to tempt ladies into his bed with a promise of marriage – the root perhaps of the later allegation that he had become betrothed to marry Eleanor.

So it was that Edward met another widow, Elizabeth, Lady Grey, the daughter of the same Richard Woodville, Lord Rivers whom he had berated as an upstart at Calais five years previously. Elizabeth first came before him to plead the restoration of her jointure from the marriage to her first husband, heir to Lord Ferrers of Groby, killed at Towton. She refused to become yet another of the king's mistresses, even – according to gossip – at the point of a dagger.[18] So driven by lust was Edward that he secretly married her on 1 May 1464. (It is, though, hard to believe that Edward was smitten by enduring love for Elizabeth: youthful passion had simply led him into a promise of a marriage too many.) He also continued his relationship with Elizabeth Lucy, who at around the same time, or a year or so later, conceived a second child of his, the future Arthur Plantagenet, Lord Lisle, whom Edward recognized as his own son.[19]

Throughout that summer of 1464, the Earl of Warwick had been negotiating a marriage alliance with the French on Edward's behalf. It was expected – and the king encouraged the policy – that he would marry a European princess as part of an international treaty. Sooner or later the truth had to be revealed and, that August, Edward acknowledged that he was indeed married. Warwick's lieutenant at Calais, Lord Wenlock, admitted in a letter to the Burgundian ambassador that, although they had accepted this *fait accompli*, the king's council and 'the great lords' were greatly (and unsurprisingly) displeased:[20] Warwick, and others, had been made to look fools. Warwick's standing as the king's indispensable right-hand man had been damaged; a major diplomatic card had been thrown away; and to make matters worse, the new queen, of only lower noble rank, was herself a widow with two children. Edward's mother, Cecily Neville – 'the right high and right excellent princess', and 'queen of right', as the Duchess of York styled herself – was reportedly equally furious. She had been close to her son in the first three years of his reign, with a role akin to that of a queen.[21] Cecily Neville was also Warwick's aunt.

Edward's clandestine marriage proved to be the pivotal event of the reign.[22] But it did not immediately lead to a rift with the Earl of Warwick, who escorted the queen in her first ceremonial appearance in September 1464 – although he was a notable absentee (as was Edward's mother) at Elizabeth's coronation on 26 May 1465. In truth, the king was always going to distance himself from his mentor at some stage; the marriage provided the occasion for him to do so. Moreover, by the middle of 1465, especially after the fugitive Henry VI had been captured in Lancashire and safely housed in the Tower, the new regime seemed at length to have established itself.

It was in these years that the glitter of the young king's court first began to come to international attention: 'the most splendid that could be found in all Christendom', the Bohemian Gabriel von Tetzel commented excessively after a visit in 1466. He described the formal re-entry to court of Queen Elizabeth after the birth of her first child with Edward, an elaborate ritual in which she was the centre of attention. The king dined less formally apart, but sumptuously. All had to kneel before him. The visitor was welcomed personally and presented with a livery collar to mark the occasion.[23]

The image of Edward as a new King Arthur was fostered. The genealogies celebrating his ancestry stressed his descent from Arthur's father, Uther Pendragon, suggesting that the dashing young man, with his Mortimer lineage, was himself the legendary 'once and future king'.[24] The first tournament of the reign of which we know took place in October 1461; another marked the short-lived reconciliation with the house of Beaufort at Whitsun 1463; and a third the coronation of Queen Elizabeth in 1465, on which occasion several Burgundian knights performed. The king himself participated in some jousts. The East Anglian knight Sir John Paston took part in a 'tourney' at Eltham in March 1467, as one of the king's team of three knights, the others being Edward's brother-in-law Anthony Woodville, Lord Scales and Thomas St Leger against a team led by Lord Hastings made up of Sir John Woodville (another brother-in-law), Sir Thomas Montgomery and John Parr. It was, Paston reported to his younger brother, 'the goodliest sight that was sene in Inglande this forty yeares'.[25]

The prominence of Queen Elizabeth's Woodville brothers as well as intimate household servants in this round of tournaments demonstrated the prominence of her family at court following her marriage to Edward and coronation. Warwick was not part of this new inner court circle and his followers were noticeably absent from its sport. He was also being displaced in royal counsels by the queen's father, Lord Rivers, who himself had been a renowned jouster in his youth. Rivers rose rapidly in favour: in 1466 he was created an earl and made treasurer of England. He manipulated a series of beneficial marriages for his family. One or two of these came directly at the Earl of Warwick's expense, as in the breaking of the contract between his nephew, George, Warwick's male heir (the son of his brother John Neville – Warwick had no sons of his own) and Anne Holland, heiress of the Duke of Exeter for the benefit of Thomas Grey, Elizabeth's oldest son by her first husband. Another marriage – of Warwick's sixty-five-year-old aunt, the widowed Duchess of Norfolk, to the queen's brother, the twenty-year-old John Woodville – was pushed through against his will. These two marriages delivered significant incomes into Woodville hands. The queen's sisters, meanwhile, were matched with the sons of the higher nobility, notably Katherine Woodville to the young Henry Stafford, Duke of Buckingham, one of the greatest heirs in the land. In allowing and encouraging these marriages, Edward had created a new faction about his person, a counterpoise to the Neville interest.[26] His jester's quip that the 'Rivers' of England ran so high that he could not wade through them, which went the rounds in 1469, struck home.[27]

The rapid rise of these new men, especially the queen's relatives, was matched by a new direction in diplomacy. France was in turmoil. In 1465 Philip, Duke of Burgundy and several great lords had risen in rebellion against the French king, Louis XI. Louis survived, but Burgundy, who held great swathes of land within the kingdom of France, from Flanders in the north to the duchy in the east as well as beyond in the German empire, was ambitious to establish an independent state of his own. In the wealthy Low Countries he had the resources to sustain his ambition. As always, French division was England's opportunity. Both France and Burgundy now courted Edward. From 1465 he played each side against the other to seek the best deal: Earl Rivers led Burgundian embassies; the Earl of Warwick negotiated with the French.[28]

The ailing Duke Philip of Burgundy, who had a long memory of the Hundred Years War, was reluctant to come to terms with England: his son and heir, Charles the Bold, was far more enthusiastic. The double diplomacy came to a head in the early summer of 1467, when two more English embassies left for the continent. The Earl of Warwick returned to France where, fêted and flattered by Louis XI, he was offered a French pension for Edward, a French marriage alliance with Edward's youngest brother Richard, and generous trading terms. But even as he negotiated, Edward was concluding a secret non-aggression pact with the Burgundian heir, Charles. Clandestine negotiations continued in England behind the cover of a long-planned tournament at Westminster on 11–15 June, a great international event in which England's champion, Anthony Woodville, Lord Scales took on Anthony, the 'bastard of Burgundy', the highly favoured illegitimate son of Duke Philip. The match ended in controversy as Scales was accused of breaking the rules; and the Anglo-Burgundian negotiations were brought to a sudden end by news of the death of Duke Philip, which brought Charles the Bold to power and transformed the diplomatic scene.

The impact on English foreign policy was immediately apparent. The French embassy, with whom the Earl of Warwick returned to England at the end of the month to present Louis XI's offer, was snubbed. Warwick, who had invested much of his prestige in pursuit of a French alliance, was scorned. Moreover in the earl's absence, on 8 June Edward had dismissed Warwick's younger brother George from the post of chancellor, personally relieving him of the Great Seal of his office. In the autumn Edward moved rapidly to conclude an alliance with Charles, the new Duke of Burgundy, involving a restoration of trading relationships which had been suspended earlier in the decade, and which was sealed by the marriage of his sister Margaret to Charles.

This diplomatic outcome was always the more likely. A triple alliance against France, with Brittany as well, was the default English alignment of the fifteenth century and commercial relationships with Flanders were central to English prosperity. But it was also a reflection of the closeness of the Woodville family to the dukes of Burgundy, for the queen's mother, Jacquetta of Luxembourg, dowager Duchess of Bedford, was a Burgundian princess. There is little doubt that Edward had been duplicitous and underhand in his dealings with the Earl of Warwick. For the second time he humiliated him in the eyes of the French. Moreover he had also removed the earl's brother and right-hand man, George Neville, from the heart of government. The events of June 1467 were, more or less, a palace coup against the earl. They marked the moment when Edward IV, now twenty-five, finally asserted his independence from his mentor and signalled the end of his reliance on the Nevilles.

4
Winter of Discontent

From the summer of 1467 relationships between the king and the Earl of Warwick began to deteriorate to the point two years later of open conflict.[1] As one commentator noted, 'they were accorded diverse times: but they never loved together after'.[2] Warwick immediately withdrew from court and retreated to his northern estates, where he remained for several months. Insults were added to injury. At the king's request a cardinal's hat was granted to Archbishop Bourchier of Canterbury, the king's cousin, rather than to Warwick's brother George Neville, who had long coveted a cardinalate, and whom Edward had only recently dismissed as chancellor. Edward refused to countenance a marriage between his brother George, Duke of Clarence and Warwick's elder daughter, Isabel. The king was not pleased subsequently to discover that, with the pair being related within the prohibited degree, the earl had secretly sought – and obtained – a dispensation from the pope for the marriage to go ahead.

More ominously for Edward, a report reached him in autumn 1467 that the earl was in treasonable communication with the Lancastrians, fostered and brokered by the cunning Louis XI, who had assiduously courted the Earl of Warwick during the abortive negotiations of the previous two years. The rumours may have been well founded; Edward, however, allowed Warwick to deny them, and did nothing further so as to avoid driving the earl into open opposition. A rapprochement was made in the spring of 1468 and the earl eventually returned to court.

Given the tense situation he had created, Edward adopted the time-honoured strategy of planning war against France as a means of restoring harmony at home. He was a model of chivalry, a proven warrior, a man in his prime. What better than to emulate Henry V? He completed the formation of a grand alliance against France, which he announced in a personal address at the opening of a new parliament in May 1468. That parliament voted him generous taxation, especially given his flamboyant promise to find all his domestic costs from his own resources. But the plans came to nothing. Louis XI quickly undermined the grand alliance by coming to an agreement with Burgundy and Brittany and by stepping up his support for Henry VI's queen Margaret of Anjou, residing in France, and dissident Lancastrians in England. In the autumn of 1468 the Earl of Warwick was once more implicated, though punishment was reserved for lesser conspirators. A plot involving the Earl of Oxford, his brother-in-law, whose father had been executed for treason in 1462, was revealed; Oxford escaped with his life, but others were executed. Disastrously, rather than reuniting his kingdom, Edward's abortive plan to invade France only led to further destabilization of his government.

By the beginning of 1469, Edward's position was

crumbling. There were several reasons for his failure, after eight years of trying, to establish himself securely on the throne. Back in 1461 he and the Earl of Warwick had promised to restore good government after the last hapless years of Henry VI's reign, but they had conspicuously failed to deliver. Popular unrest – an important element in placing Edward on the throne – was once more growing. The king, one commentator pointed out, had not brought the promised peace and prosperity, but, as he put it, much trouble and loss of goods among the common people.[3] To some extent circumstances were beyond the government's control. Recession, especially in the textile industries and towns of Wiltshire and other southern parts of the country, had continued throughout the decade; this had also held down government income through stagnant revenues from customs and excise.

Politically things were no better. The taxes that parliament had granted in 1463 and 1467 were not used to fund war against Scotland and France, but to pay general government costs. Edward's declaration in parliament that he intended to 'live of his own', entirely from the regular revenues of the crown, failed to convince his subjects. The king's coterie of Woodvilles and 'new' Yorkists at court around the figure of Earl Rivers were cast as evil ministers feathering their own nests. Moreover Edward's queen, Elizabeth Woodville – easily characterized unfairly as an unsuitable and grasping consort because of her relatively modest birth and the rapid promotion of her family – had still not produced a son. On the other hand, in exile Margaret of Anjou's son Edward was growing to manhood, while his pitiful father Henry VI remained a prisoner in the Tower. A Lancastrian restoration was always a possibility.

A disgruntled and resentful Earl of Warwick made this mixture explosive. He bided his time, dissembling reconciliation with Edward while he plotted against him. To all outward appearances, at the beginning of 1469 the king and earl were friends again. Warwick was at court; he received modest new grants, was commissioned once more to command at sea, took part in embassies and on 13 May participated in the ceremony at Windsor in which Charles the Bold was installed *in absentia* as a Knight of the Garter. At the same time he went out of his way to enhance his popularity with the people at large. Edward seems to have been taken in completely. He complacently assumed that all was back to normal and that Warwick had accepted that he was no longer the king's indispensable right-hand man. Convinced that all was well between them, early in June 1469 Edward set off on a pilgrimage to Bury St Edmunds and Walsingham.

While Edward was in East Anglia, the Earl of Warwick struck.[4] He harnessed, or maybe even orchestrated, unrest in the north. Ostensibly a popular movement, following on from earlier disturbances in Yorkshire, led by a shadowy figure named 'Robin of Redesdale', the rising was transparently a Neville rebellion. If not Warwick's steward at Middleham Castle, Sir John Conyers, the uprising's coordinator was a member of Conyers' family, while many of Warwick's northern retainers were among the rebels. Calling for reform, this army marched south.

Edward did not immediately appreciate the gravity of the

situation. The marriage of his brother George, Duke of Clarence to the Earl of Warwick's daughter Isabel also took him by surprise. With Warwick having suborned Clarence and secured the marriage dispensation in secret, he and his party slipped over to Calais, where Warwick was still Captain, under cover of going to Sandwich for the commissioning of his new flagship, *The Trinity*. There, Clarence and Isabel were married – with Warwick's brother George Neville, Archbishop of York conducting the ceremony. The Duchess of York joined them. Edward, who had mobilized troops to confront the northern rebels, seems only to have realized what was going on in Calais by early July.

On 12 July the Duke of Clarence and the Earl of Warwick themselves crossed back to Sandwich, where they issued a proclamation condemning the covetous rule of the king's evil ministers and announcing plans for reform of the common weal. Warwick called upon the same rhetoric in rebellion against Edward as he had ten years earlier against Henry VI. Raising troops as they went, they marched up to London and on to the Midlands. Edward was unusually indecisive, perhaps unwilling to accept the news of his brother's defection. While he dawdled in Nottingham, he ordered the Earls of Devon and Pembroke, Humphrey Stafford and William Herbert, to confront the forces of Robin of Redesdale. They did so at Edgecote near Banbury on 26 July and were overwhelmed. Pembroke was captured and later beheaded on Warwick's orders; Devon escaped but was captured three weeks later in Bridgwater and lynched. The queen's father, Earl Rivers, and his second son John were caught in flight in the Forest of Dean and subsequently executed. Edward, deserted by most of his men, was taken into protective custody by George Neville.

First held in Warwick Castle and then moved north to the Earl of Warwick's stronghold of Middleham, Edward was temporarily powerless. Warwick's intentions are not clear. He may have planned to rule through Edward as a puppet king, but this seems unlikely. Complacent and imprudent he may have been, but Edward was no Henry VI: he was not a man whom others could dominate or manipulate. Probably, Warwick was already intending to depose him and put Edward's brother the Duke of Clarence on the throne – a plan which later became his avowed goal. Rumours were spread for the first time that Edward was illegitimate and a parliament was summoned to meet at York in October, perhaps to change kings. But well before it convened Edward had restored his independence. The catalyst was an uprising in Northumberland by Warwick's cousins and rivals, the disinherited and disaffected senior branch of the Neville family. To act against this, the earl needed royal authorization – which was granted only on condition of the king's liberty in exchange for a guarantee of the earl's restoration to his former pre-eminence.

For six months this hollow accord survived. But the Earl of Warwick was already plotting a further rebellion; and a chastened Edward was now ever watchful. This next uprising began in Lincolnshire in March 1470, sparked by a local quarrel. Intervening immediately, Edward learned that Warwick and the Duke of Clarence were behind it, their plan being to lure him north, surprise and depose him. With all the decisiveness of which he was capable, and which he had singularly lacked six months earlier, Edward marched into the east Midlands, dealt emphatically with the rebels at Losecoat Field near Empingham and immediately closed on Warwick and Clarence. They withdrew north, then turned and fled to Devon, trying to make for Calais. An attempt by them to take Warwick's ship *The Trinity*, then docked in Southampton harbour, failed, but several of his men fell into Edward's hands. Their savage execution by impalement, carried out on Edward's behalf by the constable, John Tiptoft, Earl of Worcester, shocked contemporaries because of the method rather than the vengeful killing itself.[5] Refused entry to Calais, where Warwick's lieutenant, John, Lord Wenlock, had changed sides, the fugitives eventually landed in France and were granted refuge by Louis XI.[6]

Louis XI, ever ready to exploit an opportunity to foster civil war in England, seized the moment to effect an extraordinary reconciliation between the Earl of Warwick and Margaret of Anjou – whose husband, the Lancastrian Henry VI's reign he had overthrown less than a decade previously – solemnized at Angers in July. In a public performance Warwick abased himself before Margaret and begged for her pardon, which, with a great show of magnanimity, she granted. Her terms were that Warwick would invade England himself and restore her husband to the throne. Only when Warwick had proved his new loyalty in this way would Margaret and her son return to her kingdom. The treaty was sealed with the marriage of Warwick's younger daughter Anne to Edward, Prince of Wales, the son and heir of Henry VI and Margaret of Anjou.

Understandably, Queen Margaret could neither trust Warwick completely nor be sure that he would in fact be able to achieve this objective.

Meanwhile, that summer Edward IV took all possible precautions to prevent the Earl of Warwick's invasion, putting a fleet to sea in the Channel and defending the English coast. He had already begun the restoration of Henry Percy, whose father had been attainted after Towton, as the 4th Earl of Northumberland, to counterbalance Neville power in the north. This was now completed. He compensated John Neville with the higher title of Marquess of Montagu, the grant of forfeited estates in the West Country and the betrothal of his daughter Elizabeth (and at that time his heir) to Neville's son George. He also opened up lines of communication with the Duke of Clarence, whom Warwick by his change of coat had effectively ditched, so as ultimately to persuade him to abandon the earl.

The Earl of Warwick, however, managed to evade Edward's naval blockade. Landing in Devon that September, he marched on London. With the Lancastrian stalwarts Jasper Tudor, Earl of Pembroke and the Earl of Oxford at his right hand, and declaring that he had come to restore the rightful monarch and depose the usurping Duke of York – as he now referred to Edward – Warwick won widespread noble and popular support en route. The extent of Edward's failure to establish his regime was cruelly revealed.

As the Earl of Warwick progressed through southern England, Edward himself had been drawn north to deal with yet another Yorkshire rising instigated by Warwick's lieutenants. The north may have risen too early, but rebellion nevertheless proved an effective diversionary tactic, leaving Edward stranded in Yorkshire. Entering London unopposed, the triumphant Lancastrians released Henry VI from the Tower and placed him back on the throne. Nevertheless, Edward might still have been able to challenge Warwick had not Warwick's brother John Neville, putting family loyalty first and irritated at being deprived of the earldom of Northumberland, also deserted him. Edward was trapped between two forces, and the recently restored Earl of Northumberland was unable so soon after Towton to raise men to his cause. Therefore Edward, with the few remaining members of his household – including his brother Richard, Duke of Gloucester, his brother-in-law Anthony Woodville (who had taken his executed father's title of Earl Rivers) and his chamberlain and loyal servant Lord Hastings – made their way to the Norfolk port of Lynn where, on 2 October 1470, they commandeered a boat and escaped to Holland. The short and disastrous reign of Edward IV had apparently come to an end.

Only the previous year, the quarrel between the Earl of Warwick and Edward had been perceived as an internal dispute within the house of York, a matter of court factionalism from which the majority of the political nation held aloof. But the widespread support given to a Lancastrian restoration and the speed with which Edward's position crumbled revealed the extent of his failure. There were several reasons: internal division, and Edward's inability to rise above factional politics; the underlying weakness of the house of York from the beginning of the reign and – in spite of his shortcomings as a king – a deep residual sympathy for Henry VI; the failure of Edward's government to deliver its promise to restore peace, order and prosperity; and the young king's personal limitations. Inexperienced and naïve at the beginning of his reign, he may have left too much to his principal adherents – first the Nevilles, then the Woodvilles. Besides which he was inclined to enjoy his leisure and pleasure and leave the detail of government to others. Burgundian opinion, shared by the shrewd but undoubtedly biased Philippe de Commynes, was that his failure was his own fault, for he had shown little forethought or prudence in all his dealings with Warwick and he had been unassertive, lacking confidence in his own judgement unless supported by his closest advisers.[7]

But Edward of York was at his most decisive and formidable in a crisis. He had shown as much in 1461 when still a youth, and would reveal the same quality even more remarkably in the months that followed his flight into exile. On landing in Holland his party was given refuge by Louis de Bruges, lord of Gruthuyse, governor of the province. But Edward's arrival was an embarrassment to his brother-in-law Charles the Bold, who had given shelter to Edward's enemies the Dukes of Somerset and Exeter. That winter of 1470–71, though, the Earl of Warwick's interim Lancastrian government in Westminster took the decision to join Louis XI in an attack on Burgundy, under the terms of the treaty the French king had brokered the previous summer. Lancastrian England's declaration of war on Burgundy in January 1471 transformed Edward's fortunes. Suddenly, Charles the Bold was anxious to welcome his beloved brother-in-law to his court, and to back a Yorkist expedition to cause mischief in England. So it was that on 11 March 1471, with a motley crew of some 1,000 men, Edward set sail from the Dutch port of Veere, making first for East Anglia and then, when a landing there was denied by Lancastrian soldiers, the Yorkshire coast. It was a desperate enterprise.

Edward and his band of adventurers landed on 14 March near Ravenspur, close to Spurn Head on the Humber.[8] They headed for York, where they were admitted after Edward had sworn that he returned only for the restoration of his duchy of York, and not to attempt to regain the crown. Next they made for Wakefield, but found it difficult to raise troops from Edward's ducal estates there. However, they were not molested, either by the recently restored Earl of Northumberland, who might have had a secret understanding with Edward, or by John Neville, Marquess Montagu, who was residing in Pontefract but was unable to call upon local men – who followed the Earl of Northumberland – or mobilize in time Neville adherents further north in Yorkshire. After Wakefield, Edward turned south through the east Midlands and was reinforced by troops answering a call to arms from Lord Hastings, as well as men brought in from Cumbria by Sir William Parr, both senior officers in Edward's household. As the swelling army marched south it was shadowed by the combined forces of the Duke of Exeter, the Earl of Oxford and Montagu, but they failed to challenge him. He stopped to celebrate Mass at Daventry on Palm Sunday, 7 April. There, the boards concealing an image of St Anne that had been closed for Lent miraculously opened to reveal her.[9] This was, the official account of the campaign later declared, a portent of his ultimate triumph.

The Lancastrian strategy was to gather overwhelming strength in Warwickshire and there to crush Edward: the Earl of Warwick, based in Coventry, recruited men in the name of Henry VI. The Duke of Clarence marched with reinforcements from the West Country. However, on 3 April, three miles out of Warwick, Clarence joined forces not with his father-in-law Warwick, but with his brother. Edward's secret wooing of Clarence through the women of their family, including their mother, over the previous months had been successful. Edward and Clarence immediately challenged Warwick to battle but, ever cautious, he declined. So Edward made for London, where he took custody of Henry VI in the Tower – who cut a pitiful figure when he was paraded in an attempt to rally London to his cause – was reunited with his queen and was presented with his son and heir, who had been born in sanctuary in Westminster the previous November. By now Warwick, all his remaining forces mustered, was heading for London.

The two armies finally met north of London at Barnet in thick fog on 14 April, Easter Day. In a battle more confused and confusing than most, Edward led from the front. The author of *The Arrivall* (the official account of Edward's campaign written later in the year) described how in the battle, trusting in God's help, Our Blessed Lady and St George, he

> manly vigorously and valiantly assailed them [the enemy] in
> the midst and strongest of their battle [formation], where

he, with great violence beat and bore down before him all that stood in his way, and then turned to range, first on that one hand, and then on the other hand, so that nothing might stand in the sight of him.[10]

Edward carried the day. The Earl of Warwick's brother, John Neville, Marquess of Montagu, was killed in the mêlée; the Duke of Exeter, left for dead, was later taken prisoner. The Earl of Oxford managed to escape. Warwick was caught and cut down as he tried to flee. Thus ended the tortuous career of the great earl known to posterity as the Kingmaker. Edward was finally rid of him. Greatly admired by his contemporaries and for several generations to come, Warwick has not enjoyed a high reputation among modern historians because of his destabilizing impact on the kingdom.

On the same day as Edward's victory at Barnet, Margaret of Anjou finally landed at Weymouth with her son, the seventeen-year-old Lancastrian heir Edward. She was joined by Edmund Beaufort, Duke of Somerset and John Courtenay, Earl of Devon, and marched north to link up with the Earl of Pembroke advancing from Wales, all three stalwart opponents of the Yorkists. But, back in London, Edward immediately raised new recruits and without hesitation rapidly marched to intercept her before she could cross the Severn for the safety of Wales. On 4 May he caught up with her army outside Tewkesbury. Edward's bold frontal attack and astute tactical awareness once again assured victory in a battle in which his youngest brother, Richard of Gloucester, distinguished himself. Edward of Lancaster was captured, possibly in flight, and cold-bloodedly killed; the Duke of Somerset and other leaders were dragged out of Tewkesbury Abbey where they had claimed sanctuary and, notwithstanding the king's promise to pardon them, executed after a cursory trial before a constable's court over which Richard of Gloucester presided.[11]

Even then, Edward faced more threats. Heading into the Midlands to confront another uprising, this time in northern Yorkshire, he had reached Coventry before learning that the rebels had been dispersed. In the south-east, London was under threat from a force raised in Kent and led by the Bastard of Fauconberg, George Neville, the illegitimate son of the Earl of Warwick's uncle, Lord Fauconberg, who had long served him. The Bastard Fauconberg had been patrolling the Channel as admiral of Warwick's fleet. Commanded by Earl Rivers and the Earl of Essex, the city held firm and Fauconberg's attack was repulsed. When on 18 May news of Edward's approach reached London, Fauconberg withdrew.

Edward entered London on 21 May. It was rumoured that the Earl of Warwick's brother Archbishop George Neville, who had had the care of Henry VI, had secretly undertaken to prevent the Lancastrian king taking sanctuary in Westminster a month earlier; Neville certainly succeeded in making his own peace with Edward. However, that same night Henry VI was put to death on Edward's orders, probably by his brother Richard of Gloucester, according to a contemporary, 'being then at the Tower'.[12] He had only been kept alive after his capture in 1465 because his son and heir had been safe in France and would have proved a more potent threat as the true, Lancastrian, 'Edward IV'. Edward of Lancaster's death sealed his father's fate. The direct line of the house of Lancaster was finally eradicated; Warwick had at last been overthrown. Edward had disposed of almost all his enemies. Moreover, his own son and heir had been born. The happy reunion of father, wife and son was publicized and victory celebrated in a great round of public thanksgiving to God. He who had dared, had won.

Contemporaries were astonished by Edward's change of fortune. *The Arrivall*, produced for circulation in Burgundy and France, stressed the overwhelming odds he had overcome and the martial prowess he had displayed. It was indeed a remarkable comeback, achieved partly through divisions among his enemies which enabled him to take them on separately; partly through his cunning in neutralizing the Earl of Northumberland and winning back his brother Clarence, whose timely switch of sides had sealed the Earl of Warwick's fate; but above all by his own strategic and tactical brilliance. He had acted quickly and decisively throughout. He had out-thought and out-manoeuvred his enemies at every stage. He had once more demonstrated his personal ability in battle by leading from the front and inspiring his men to take on his enemies in direct hand-to-hand combat. This was a new beginning for Edward: he was now able to rule England from a far stronger position than he had ever enjoyed before 1470. The winter of discontent was over.

5
Master of All His Foes

By the end of May 1471 Edward had recovered his throne, eliminated the direct Lancastrian line and destroyed the Earl of Warwick. Nevertheless, it took time for him to eradicate all opposition and to regain full command of the kingdom. The first task was to pacify Kent, Sussex and the Cinque Ports, which had long been favourable to Warwick and risen again in his cause. A few prominent men were executed, and a royal commission imposed swingeing fines on all those who were implicated. As one commentator put it, those not hanged by the neck were hanged by the purse;[1] another noted that the king had out of Kent much good and little love.[2]

Calais, the Earl of Warwick's bastion, held out until July when it surrendered to John, Lord Howard, one of Edward's most trusted household servants. Jasper Tudor, Earl of Pembroke was at large in west Wales until September. Recognizing his isolation, he sailed for refuge in Brittany, taking with him his young nephew Henry, the future Henry VII, who through his mother Margaret Beaufort, sister of the Duke of Somerset executed after Tewkesbury, was a tenuous Lancastrian claimant to the throne.[3] More persistent resistance came from the Earl of

Oxford, who escaped first to Scotland, then France. In April 1472 Oxford was harassing the Marches of Calais in collusion with George Neville, Archbishop of York, his brother-in-law. Neville was arrested and imprisoned at Hammes, one of the forts guarding the approaches to Calais. Ever alert to financial benefit, Edward seized, allegedly by trickery, the archbishop's considerable wealth.[4] In the spring of 1473, with ships provided by Louis XI, Oxford sailed once more for Scotland but, not finding a welcome there, tried an abortive landing in Essex. After a spell of piracy in the English Channel, in September he sailed to St Michael's Mount off the south coast of Cornwall where, besieged by Edward's men, he held out until February 1474, when he was abandoned by his men, who were offered pardons. Oxford's life was spared, but he was sent to join Neville in indefinite captivity at Hammes.[5] Edward was at last, as one of the laments after his death declared, 'master of all his foes'.[6]

There were relatively few new attainders. Henry Holland, Duke of Exeter, a residual heir of the house of Lancaster who had survived Barnet, was kept a prisoner in the Tower. On the other hand, several of the more able civil servants who had remained loyal to Lancaster and had shared exile finally made their peace with Edward's regime and joined royal service. Prominent among those who now concluded that the cause of Lancaster was irretrievably lost were John Morton, Bishop of Ely and the senior judge John Fortescue.

The main reason why there were few attainders and confiscations of the estates of Lancastrians and Neville

followers in 1471 was that the principal rebel, the Earl of
Warwick himself, was not condemned. It seems that con-
fiscation of the Warwick inheritance was at first intended.
It did not proceed because the king wished to bestow it on
his brothers, and his brothers demanded of him terms that
were stronger than a mere royal grant at the king's pleasure of the lands of a condemned traitor. There followed a
long-drawn-out squabble, out of which none of the three
emerged with much credit. In law, the half that the earl
had held of his countess Anne's inheritance as the heir to
the Beauchamp Earls of Warwick, from whom he had
derived his title, still belonged to his widow for the rest of
her life. As the earl's own Neville estates had not been confiscated on account of his treason, the half that he had
inherited from his father should have descended through
the legal device of 'tail male', through which the lands pass
to the nearest male heir of the deceased. This was Warwick's nephew, George, Duke of Bedford (still a boy).
Legal niceties such as these were no impediment to a king
resolved to reward his brothers with the partition of Warwick's inheritance. At first Edward granted the whole of
the Beauchamp half to the Duke of Clarence, husband of
the countess's daughter, Isabel. Richard of Gloucester was
granted the northern Neville estates.[7]

But Edward's youngest brother wanted more. Gaining
Edward's approval for his marriage to Warwick's younger
daughter, Anne, Richard of Gloucester claimed an equal
share of the Beauchamp inheritance. Despite Edward's
entreaties, Clarence refused to part with any of it. He was
reported as conceding that his brother could have the girl – in

his care at the time – but none of the livelihood.[8] A compromise was reached. Gloucester married Anne in July 1472. Her mother Anne, Countess of Warwick was cowering in sanctuary in Beaulieu Abbey, appealing desperately for her rights to be upheld. Eventually Gloucester answered her plea, only to convey her in July 1473 to Middleham, where she was held in virtual house arrest until Richard met his death at Bosworth in 1485. The kidnapping of the Countess of Warwick led to an immediate worsening in the relationships between the brothers. In the autumn it was reported that Clarence 'maketh him big' so as to deal once and for all with his little brother.[9] He may even have been in communication with the Earl of Oxford at St Michael's Mount.[10]

Edward finally stepped in and imposed a settlement, the validity of which relied solely on acts of parliament passed in 1474 and 1475. In the first the Countess Anne was disinherited and declared legally dead, and her estates partitioned between her daughters. In the other the young Duke of Bedford was disinherited and his rights to the Neville inheritance, which Richard of Gloucester had occupied since 1471 by royal grant, were now formally conveyed to him by statute. In time Bedford joined the dowager Countess of Warwick as an unwilling guest at Middleham. In effect the Warwick inheritance came to be partitioned between Clarence in the south and Gloucester in the north. The acts rode roughshod over the laws of inheritance. The proceedings and behaviour of the three brothers dismayed the Crowland chronicler, who preferred not to write about them in detail when he came to compose his memoirs.[11]

The division of Warwick's estates, flagrantly unjust as it was, fitted the shape of the political regime Edward now began to construct. He would rule England's regions through his family and core household men, who would control the provinces on his behalf. Richard of Gloucester was to dominate the north. The Earl of Warwick's extensive following of local gentry, household and estate staff and tenants, some formally bound to him by life contracts of service and in receipt of fees, passed with barely a pause into Gloucester's service. Initial tensions with two great regional powers, the Bishop of Durham and Earl of Northumberland, were resolved by 1474. Lord Stanley, an experienced politician who had since 1459 turned the practice of trimming his political sails into an art, continued to hold sway in Lancashire and Cheshire. Edward took the opportunity of a progress to Shrewsbury in August 1473, where his second son Richard was born, to enhance the powers of a council based at Ludlow, first created as an advisory body for the upbringing of his baby son Edward, Prince of Wales and Earl of March. As the young prince's governor, his uncle Anthony, Earl Rivers was granted authority to administer the prince's estates and exercise royal authority in his name. Clarence commanded the Midlands and the West Country, though Lord Hastings and Lord Dinham, steward to the duchy of Cornwall, also played a significant role respectively in each region. There was no master plan; the shape of the regime emerged and changed by trial and error and according to political expediency. But the framework was clear. Provincial England was to be ruled through those that the king believed he could trust to hold the kingdom unswervingly for him.[12]

Lawlessness was still a problem. Complaints continued, in parliament and by petition directly to the king, of murderers going unpunished because of the support of influential lords. The general level of disorder was a matter of concern to the Commons in the parliament that met between 1472 and 1475, especially in Shropshire and Herefordshire. During this parliament, as at others, legislation was promoted by the Commons to improve the administration of the law. Edward heard cases in person in council. He attended and addressed parliament, scrutinized some of the legislation and oversaw the implementation of some statutes, especially the Act of Resumption of 1473, by which royal estates granted to subjects could be brought back into hand. This was primarily a review of patronage rather than a financial re-entrenchment, although Edward refused to renew a grant of the duchy of Lancaster lordship of Tutbury to Clarence. But Edward's capacity to enforce law and order, especially over his more powerful subjects, who were able to pervert the course of justice through intimidation or bribery, was limited. He is known to have intervened in disputes which threatened major disorder, such as over the possession of Hornby Castle in Lancashire in 1473 in which Richard of Gloucester and Lord Stanley took opposite sides. For the most part, however, the oversight of justice in the provinces through assizes and quarter sessions was left more informally, for good or ill, to local lords.

*

The tensions within the Yorkist establishment in the early 1470s, let alone the need to win over those whose sympathies still lay with the defeated house of Lancaster, provided an even more powerful incentive than in 1468 to secure inward peace and unity through outward war with France. Besides, as far as Edward was concerned, there was unfinished business to settle with the French king, Louis XI, who had played a key role in the Earl of Warwick's pro-Lancastrian coup against him in 1470. Between 1471 and 1475 preparations for an invasion of France, this time with serious intent, dominated Edward's policy-making.

First the diplomatic groundwork had to be undertaken.[13] The king set out to renew his offensive alliances with Brittany and Burgundy, as well as to secure the neutrality of other powers. All this entailed long-drawn-out negotiations. Key to his plans was the alliance with his brother-in-law Charles the Bold of Burgundy, who had after all assisted him to recover his throne. But Duke Charles had other ambitions and was at heart unwilling to run the risk of making war on Louis XI except in defence of his territories. Edward sent several embassies to him; all returned empty-handed. Edward had greater initial success in his dealings with the Hanse and Scots, so as to secure the seas on the one hand and his northern border on the other. Since 1468 a low-key war at sea had been pursued with the Hanseatic League, a confederation of German and Baltic ports, but after exhaustive negotiations a peace was concluded in February 1474 on terms largely favourable to the Hanse. In October that year, an Anglo-Scottish treaty of perpetual peace was agreed between the two kingdoms, to be sealed by the marriage of Edward's daughter Cecily to the heir to the Scottish throne, the future James IV. By this time Charles the Bold had at last agreed to a formal offensive alliance against Louis XI, under which Edward undertook to land in France by 1 July 1475. Finally, in the early summer of 1475 Brittany confirmed its alliance, and treaties were concluded with Castile and Denmark to secure their neutrality.

In the meantime Edward had been raising taxes to pay for an army. This was the main purpose for calling the parliament that first met at Westminster in October 1472. In the traditional opening address to the assembly, the chancellor declared Edward's intention to recover his rightful throne of France and retake possession of the duchies of Normandy and Guyenne. He urged his audience to 'consider the knightly courage, great prowess and disposition of our Sovereign Lord the King' as supremely fitted for the task.[14] Moreover, the campaign would, he claimed, using the customary rhetoric, bring law, order and peace at home and secure the English Channel for merchant shipping.[15] To this end the House of Commons was asked to vote for supply.

Following a precedent of 1453, it offered an income tax to pay for a force of 13,000 archers for six months, which was expected to raise over £118,000, four times the yield of the conventional subsidy, a tax of a tenth and fifteenth. But, mindful of Edward's form in 1463 and 1468 – taking the taxes and failing to spend them on the war for which they had been voted – the Commons ruled that it should be held in special repositories and not released until the army was mustered.

The yield fell far short of expectations. In consequence Edward set out to discover what his subjects would be prepared to give him for his expedition 'by way of their good will and benevolence' – donations which it was difficult for his principal subjects to refuse and from which he raised a further £21,000.[16] In the winter of 1474–5 he personally toured East Anglia to help raise the money, charming his subjects to open their purses; it was later said that one Suffolk widow doubled her contribution after he kissed her.[17] Nevertheless by early 1475, even with the capacity to raise loans on the security of the taxation, there was still not enough in the war chest. Parliament grudgingly granted a further conventional subsidy.

Appropriately for one preparing to go to war, Edward also attended to matters pertaining to his soul. In 1473 he appointed William Beauchamp, Bishop of Salisbury master and surveyor of his new works at Windsor. On 12 June 1475, shortly before he set off for France, he formally instructed Beauchamp 'to build and construct a new chapel in honour of the blessed St Mary and St George the Martyr within our Castle of Windsor'.[18] He also drew up his will. It was mainly concerned with instructions for his tomb in the new chapel at Windsor should he die on campaign. He also settled significant parts of the duchies of Lancaster and York on trustees to pay his debts, provide an apanage for his younger son and to pay marriage portions for his daughters.

Recruitment of the army, as well as the stockpiling of armaments (especially artillery) and supplies and the requisitioning of transport to convey the force across the Channel, began in the summer of 1474. Almost the entire royal household was mobilized, most of the great lords recruiting their own contingents. Including non-combatants, the army of 20,000 was one of the largest to cross the Channel in the fifteenth century. All was ready by the beginning of June 1475, and troops began to sail to Calais on the 7th. The whole operation took three weeks. On 20 June a regency government was established under the nominal rule of the five-year-old Prince of Wales. Edward himself crossed on 4 July.

Over four years Edward, in conjunction with his council, had driven forward the preparations for war, single-mindedly coordinating the preparation for this invasion. The king and his council had laid the diplomatic groundwork, raised the taxes and recruited the army; and they had done so on schedule for the agreed deadline of 1 July 1475. It was an impressive achievement. Yet in the event it all came to very little.

The first and crucial setback was that Charles the Bold failed to honour his agreement.[19] He had been drawn into a long siege of Neuss on the Rhine to the east of his duchy of Gelders within the Holy Roman Empire, and only returned to Flanders in June, where he remained. Without the expected Burgundian support, Edward's army moved cautiously from Calais, through Burgundian-held Picardy, reaching Peronne on the Somme on 5 August. All the time Edward was waiting for Burgundy to mobilize, which it failed to do. Neither did Edward's other ally, Brittany. On the other hand a powerful French army under Louis XI was bearing down on Edward. He could have fought, but his army was untried, deserted by its allies and not fully equipped for open battle.

Given the circumstances, it did not take long for Edward to open peace negotiations with Louis. Terms were swiftly agreed. Louis accepted most of the English demands: a payment of £15,000 immediately and thereafter £10,000 a year; a marriage alliance between his son and heir the Dauphin and Edward's eldest daughter Elizabeth; trade concessions and a seven-year truce. It was in fact remarkably similar to the terms offered by Louis XI to the Earl of Warwick in 1467, and cost him comparatively little. The treaty was sealed by the two kings in person, on a specially constructed bridge over the River Somme at Picquigny on 29 August.[20] In the meantime the city of Amiens was opened to the English troops to enjoy themselves at French expense and most of Edward's commanders accepted sweeteners from Louis – some openly, some secretly. The English army, no doubt somewhat the worse for wear, began to drift home from Calais on 4 September; Edward set sail on 18 September. During the return crossing of the Channel the Duke of Exeter, who had been released from the Tower to join the king, fell overboard – or, if the Milanese ambassador to the court of Burgundy is to be believed, Edward had him thrown into the sea.[21] Edward entered London on the 28th. There was no triumphal welcome home.

It was a sad anticlimax to Edward's Great Enterprise – and was not what he had had in mind. He had not set off to France with such a large army with the intention of being paid off without a shot being fired. Although it was said that Edward's foremost herald, Garter King of Arms, had indicated in an embassy to Louis at the eleventh hour that the king was willing to negotiate,[22] this was, even if true, conventional diplomacy. The collapse of the triple alliance with Burgundy and Brittany undermined the expedition. To have fought alone would have been folly. Unlike the triumphant Henry V in 1415 or 1417, Edward was not invading a deeply divided France but was facing a powerful and seasoned army. The alliance's strategy might have been to lay siege to one or two towns, perhaps secure them and then negotiate an honourable peace. In the event not even this was feasible.

Edward did his best to claim that the campaign's outcome fully justified the expense and effort. He represented the treaty as a 'victory without stroke' and described his annual pension as tribute paid by a defeated enemy.[23] Whether pension or tribute, it would obviate the need for future taxation; the return over several years would recover what had been spent. Edward therefore graciously declined the instalment of the last subsidy that had not yet been levied. The commercial clauses of the Treaty of Picquigny benefited England's mercantile community. However, not all his subjects were convinced by the spin Edward put on the campaign's outcome. There were disturbances in Hampshire and Wiltshire, for which demobilized soldiers were blamed.[24] But Edward's control of his kingdom was not weakened by the failure to win glory in France.

6

The Sun in Splendour

Commynes noted that when he saw Edward at Picquigny in 1475, this once handsome man was beginning to go to seed. He had looked, he judged, at his best in 1470.[1] The likeness in the Royal Collection, with 'the bovine and lack-lustre features which peer blearily'[2] at us, made in the early 1470s, might capture the beginning of this physical deterioration. Nevertheless, now in his mid thirties, he had all the appearance of a model monarch ruling his kingdom with verve and authority. He had pursued the ultimate princely purpose of going to war, and – in his own version, at any rate – had returned with honour. His kingdom too was internally more at peace and prosperity was at last returning. Economic revival and industrial expansion were discernible that would continue for half a century. William Caxton set up his first printing press in Westminster in 1476 to sell books to a new, wider market. New schools promoted the revived classical learning, the first Atlantic exploration was launched, the clothing industries of the West Country, the West Riding and East Anglia boomed, and parish churches were refashioned in the current Perpendicular style. There was some foundation to Thomas More's nostalgia for a golden age at the time of his birth in 1478.

Edward now had the leisure to fulfil one outstanding family duty: the reburial with full funeral rites of his father in the family mausoleum at Fotheringhay in Northamptonshire. This great state event, in the summer of 1476, was a dynastic ceremony designed to demonstrate the unbreakable unity of Edward's family and the unchallengeable hold of the house of York on the throne. The bodies of Richard of York and his second son Edmund, who had fallen at Wakefield at the end of 1460 and been buried at nearby Pontefract, were exhumed on 21 July. After a requiem Mass a magnificent cortège, accompanied by the principal nobles of the realm led by Richard of Gloucester, and including 400 men on foot chanting prayers, processed solemnly in a week-long journey to Fotheringhay where it was met by the king, queen and Duke of Clarence. The reburial, marked by another requiem Mass, took place on 30 July followed by a gargantuan banquet. The house of York, the world was to understand, was here to stay as the true ruling dynasty of England, united and secure in its hold on the throne.[3]

In these years Edward's court, 'such as befitted a mighty kingdom filled with riches', was at its most magnificent. It was heavily influenced by the style and etiquette of Burgundy, the most flamboyant ruling house in northern Europe, which he had observed during his exile.[4] In part the splendour of the court reflected the king's liking for show and conspicuous consumption; in part it was a public display of power designed to underscore his total command. The court, the political, social and cultural hub of the kingdom, was inhabited not only by the leading

1. Dame Fortune turns her wheel to raise a king from the dust and then topple him – something she did twice in the case of Edward IV and his sons.

2. Edward was an enthusiastic jouster and promoter of tournaments. This detail of a famous early-fifteenth-century joust comes from 'The Beauchamp Pageant', a manuscript probably completed by Warwick the Kingmaker's widow, Anne, c.1485–90.

3. Edward did not hesitate to kill captured prisoners. In this near-contemporary representation of the beheading of Edmund Beaufort, Duke of Somerset, the king looks on approvingly as Somerset, dragged out of sanctuary after the Battle of Tewkesbury, is executed.

4. Bishop John Alcock, tutor to Edward's son and heir the Prince of Wales, commissioned a window at Little Malvern Priory in honour of the king and his family. This detail shows Edward's queen, Elizabeth Woodville, and three of their daughters.

5. Garter stall plate of William, Lord Hastings, in St George's Chapel, Windsor. Head of the king's household, Hastings was Edward's boon companion and loyal servant to the death.

his boke late translate here in syght
By Antony Erle   that vertuous knyght
Please it to accepte to youre noble grace
And at youre conuenient leysoure and space
It to see rede and vnderstond
A precious Iewell for alle youre lond

6. Anthony Woodville, Earl Rivers, presents a copy of 'The Dictes and Sayings of the Philosophers' to Edward who, arrayed in full regalia, is accompanied by his queen and heir.

7. This early Tudor portrait of Edward, based on an original believed to have been painted in the early 1470s, reveals that by the time he was just over thirty years old, the king had lost the early bloom of youth.

8. Edward IV's badges of a sun in splendour and a white rose decorate the inside cover of this alabaster-relief altarpiece, which depicts the head of John the Baptist. Dating from *c.*1471–83, the altarpiece was possibly commissioned by a member of the royal household.

9. Edward IV's tomb at St George's Chapel, Windsor, was never completed. He was buried under the most easterly arch of the north aisle, close to the altar. Iron gates, which now close off the arch, were installed by 1484.

members and officers of his household, but also by great nobles who were not of the household. They came and went according to their other commitments. A core, including Lord Hastings, the queen's son Thomas Grey, Marquess of Dorset and her brother Sir Edward Woodville, were frequently in attendance and formed an intimate coterie about the king. It was the stage for great occasions of state, conducted according to strict etiquette, but also the playground in which the king relaxed with his boon companions.

The king entertained lavishly, treating guests with a nicely judged balance of formality and ease. In 1472 Louis of Gruthuyse was entertained by the king at Windsor when he was created Earl of Winchester in gratitude for his hospitality two years earlier during Edward's exile. This was a more relaxed occasion, which involved dancing in the evening, Mass the next morning followed by hunting in the park, then a formal banquet after which there was more dancing, and at the end of the day the king and queen accompanied their guest to his elaborately and lavishly decorated apartments.[5]

Edward made the most of his imposing height and handsome appearance. He still cut, the Crowland chronicler recalled fondly, an incomparable figure. His magnificent dress impressed observers. The wardrobe accounts of 1480 reveal the lavish materials – cloth of gold, satin, damask, velvet, sable and ermine – used to make up the twenty-six gowns, doublets and jackets, let alone the dozens of shoes, boots, hats and other clothes supplied that year. He loved to show himself off in all his finery. In addition he amassed a huge collection of jewellery.[6] Royal residences, especially Eltham where he built a new great hall, were modernized in these years. Crowland believed that their furnishings outstripped anything seen before, being adorned with Arras tapestries, other hangings and cushions and lavishly supplied with gold, silver and plate.[7]

In the last ten years of his life Edward also commissioned and collected over thirty expensive and exquisitely illuminated manuscripts and early printed books, histories, chivalric romances and didactic works. All were produced in Flanders but elaborately bound in England. The inspiration for his library, too, was Burgundian – perhaps specifically the library possessed by Gruthuyse, a noted bibliophile. Book-collecting in the fifteenth century was not just a private passion, or designed for impressive display, though both of these motives were no doubt present in Edward's purchases. The books themselves are large and were probably used for readings from a lectern at court, possibly after dinner, when on other occasions music was performed and dancing took place.[8]

Christian observance was also deployed as part of this display, as well as an element of political calculation.[9] The births of children and the marriage of his own son Richard in 1478 were marked by full and elaborate ceremony. Although Crowland claimed that Edward was 'a Catholic of the strongest faith, a stalwart enemy of heretics, and most devoted venerator of the Church's sacraments',[10] other evidence suggests that his own religious devotion was little more than conventional and his observance routine. As did all kings, he maintained a royal chapel, staffed with chaplains – essentially a department of his household.

The chapel royal was the centre of English musical tradition and in particular the development of polyphony in the fifteenth century, which he continued by the appointment of 'gentlemen-clerks' to enhance the singing. He heard Mass once a day in the chapel; on particular feast days, such as All Saints, Christmas and Easter, there were special Masses, and on Sundays during Lent he and his family heard sermons preached by eminent divines. He distributed alms in the form of wine to the family mausoleum at Fotheringhay, other royal foundations and various religious institutions. He made modest grants to the Sheen Charterhouse and was a benefactor of the Brigettine House across the river at Syon. His only foundation was the first house of the Observant Franciscans in England at Greenwich. He rarely went on pilgrimage: to Bury St Edmund's and Walsingham in 1469 and two years later to Canterbury. He is never recorded to have touched for the King's Evil, the power supposedly accorded to kings to cure scrofula.

Edward's special saint was St George, already perceived as the national saint of England, and the focus of his devotion the chapel dedicated to that saint at Windsor, which he intended to rebuild. The first work, undertaken on his return from France, was a chantry in which his body was to be laid in the north-east corner of the existing building. This was completed by 1481. Work began on the new walls of the main structure in 1477 and continued rapidly thereafter, ready for roofing to begin in 1480. In 1481 a new charter was given to the college, which increased the number of clerks and choristers to twenty-six. The fifty stalls in which the Garter Knights and canons were to sit were in place by the end of 1482. By the time of Edward's death the eastern arm was almost finished. But his tomb was still not ready. Work then stopped, to be renewed by Henry VII in 1492.[11] Edward shunned Westminster Abbey because of its Lancastrian associations: it housed Henry V's tomb, and Henry VI had planned to be buried there too. By transforming the chapel of the Order of the Garter into a mausoleum for his dynasty he made an unambiguous statement that he saw himself as the true and legitimate successor of Edward III.

St George's was the spiritual home of the Order of the Garter which Edward III had founded in 1348. Edward IV promoted the order in conscious rivalry with the Duke of Burgundy's Order of the Golden Fleece. He attended the annual feasts at Windsor whenever he could; when he could not, the chapters of the order, at which new members were elected and the statutes amended, were held wherever he was residing on 23 April. Like the Order of the Golden Fleece, of which Edward became a member in 1468, vacancies were deployed for diplomatic ends as well as for recognition of chivalric achievement, starting with his brother-in-law Charles the Bold in 1469 and continuing later in the reign with King Ferdinand of Aragon, King João of Portugal and Ercole d'Este, Duke of Ferrara.[12]

While early in his reign Edward participated vigorously in tournaments, later we may suspect he was a sponsor and spectator. In this his grandson, Henry VIII, took after him. Tournaments and jousting were originally designed as training for war, but there was very little of this element in Edwardian tournaments; during his reign they became court spectacle. Edward was represented as the model of chivalry: he had been victorious in every battle in which he fought. Yet as events in the 1460s and again in 1475 showed, Edward was a reluctant warrior, fighting only when absolutely necessary – unlike Henry V and before him Edward III, with whom he preferred to be identified, who were natural soldiers who revelled in fighting. As Commynes observed, 'he was not cut out to endure all the toil'.[13]

Edward was a man of natural charm, 'of gentle nature and cheerful aspect'.[14] Dominic Mancini, the Italian visitor who was received at court at the end of 1482 or in early 1483, recorded what must surely have been his personal experience:

> He was so genial in his greeting that if he saw a newcomer bewildered at his appearance and royal magnificence he would give him courage to speak by laying a kindly hand upon his shoulder.[15]

Edward's informality when 'off duty' struck several commentators as unusual, reflecting perhaps his upbringing as a young nobleman rather than as the heir to the throne. He was not a king who aloofly kept his distance from his subjects. He appears to have been a man who had a magnetic personal appeal. However, as Mancini also recorded, he had a fearful temper.

After 1475 Edward confined himself largely to the Thames valley, moving between Westminster, Sheen, Eltham and Windsor, with an occasional visit to his

Oxfordshire manor of Woodstock for hunting. He now devoted himself even more to the pursuit of the pleasures in which, according to Philippe de Commynes, no man ever took more delight and to which he became addicted. 'He thought of nothing else but women (far more than is reasonable), hunting and feasting.'[16] Crowland observed the self-indulgence of 'a gross man addicted to conviviality [feasting], vanity, drunkenness, extravagance and passion' at close quarters.[17] Mancini heard that 'in food and drink he was most immoderate' and would 'take an emetic for the delight of gorging his stomach once more'.[18]

Edward's lifestyle may well have had a deletereous effect on his health. Throughout his reign he consulted alchemists and astrologers, both closely bound up with the practice of medicine. He spent heavily on medicines and fumigations, particularly to ward off the plague. In 1479 there was a severe outbreak which possibly carried off his two-year-old son George. Withdrawing to Eltham and Sheen, he secured a dispensation from the pope to eat meat during Lent so as to keep up his strength. It was possibly at this time too that a special medicine was prepared 'for the king's grace' to be taken daily to protect him from the 'reigning sickness'. If so, its ingredients of rue, marigolds, burnet, sorrel and other herbs proved surprisingly effective.[19]

Edward also had an excessive sexual appetite. He had three identifiable mistresses and at least three, possibly five, identifiable illegitimate children.[20] By 1475 Elizabeth Lambert, the wife of a London merchant, later known as Mistress Shore, seems to have had something of the status of an official mistress. But a chorus of gossip, repeated by More, Mancini and Commynes, salivated over Edward's insatiability. More joked about three mistresses, 'the merriest, the wiliest and the holiest' harlots in his realm. Shore was the merriest; he did not name the other two, who were higher-born.[21]

In his history of Richard III, More stated that the 'fleshly wantonness' of Edward's youth had abated by the later years of his life and he asserted that the king took his pleasure without violence.[22] More darkly, he had the Duke of Buckingham, speaking on behalf of Richard III's claim to the throne, say that there was

no woman ... young or old, rich or poor, whom he [Edward] set his eye upon ... but without any fear of God or respect of his honour, murmur or grudge of the world, he would importunately pursue his appetite and have her to the great destruction of many a good woman.[23]

Writing just after Edward's death, Mancini said almost the same. He commented that Edward was licentious in the extreme:

It was said he had been most abusive to numerous women after he had seduced them, for as soon as he grew weary of dalliance he gave up the ladies much against their will to the other courtiers; he pursued with no discrimination the married and the unmarried, the noble and lowly. However he took none by force. He overcame all by money and promises, and having conquered them, he dismissed them.[24]

'The companions of his vice', he added, included Edward's close associate and chamberlain Lord Hastings, the queen's sons by her first marriage (Sir Thomas Grey, Marquess of Dorset and Sir Richard Grey) and her brother Sir Edward Woodville.[25]

This image of the debauchery of Edward's court would seem also to underlie a passage in the *Titulus Regius* (Richard III's recital of his right to the throne advanced in 1483 and enacted by parliament in 1484), which condemns Edward's regime. 'The land was ruled by self will and pleasure,' and among other things 'no man was sure of his wife, daughter or servant, every good maiden and woman standing in dread to be ravished and defouled'.[26] Edward is not mentioned by name – indeed it purports to describe the kingdom as a whole – but the passage is but a veiled reference to Edward's own behaviour, the rule of his own self-will and pleasure.

This may be dismissed as malicious character assassination on a par with the other hint in the *Titulus Regius* that Edward IV was himself a bastard. Even if this were so, it is likely that gossip about Edward's treatment of women was already in circulation and believed. Richard of Gloucester would have known what went on at court. From these testimonies, while only the *Titulus Regius* implies rape, Edward IV does not emerge as the harmless philanderer Thomas More airily condoned, and has generally – and indulgently – been taken to be.

Queen Elizabeth had no choice but to accept his behaviour. Indeed she continued regularly to give birth to children after Edward's recovery of the throne in 1471:

Richard in 1473, Anne in 1475, George in 1477 (he died aged two), Katherine in 1479 and Bridget in 1480. She had twelve children in all, ten to Edward, the last born when she was forty-two. She has tended to suffer a bad press in modern times. This stems from the hostility of Warwick the Kingmaker and later of Richard III, both of whom accused her of witchcraft and of exercising excessive influence over the king. In truth Elizabeth fulfilled her role, including the production of numerous children, with propriety and discretion. She was a modest patron of the Church, adding to the endowment of Queens' College, Cambridge. While she may well have promoted the interests of her family, her supposedly malign influence over Edward, against which Warwick and Richard III railed, was in fact exercised by her male relations, whom Edward rather than she herself indulged. In 1472 the Speaker in the House of Commons praised her womanly behaviour and great constancy during Edward IV's exile when, in sanctuary at Westminster, she gave birth to Edward, Prince of Wales. She appears to have adopted an illegitimate child of one of Edward's liaisons, Grace, who was present at her funeral.[27] Crowland drew attention to Edward's love of his family, of which his queen was the centre, and the unusual prominence given to his children at court.[28] This carefully crafted public image of the happy family sits uncomfortably alongside the debauchery behind the scenes. Indoors the sun shone less brightly.

The image of one united ruling dynasty, so carefully fostered by the reburial of Edward's father in 1476, was soon shattered. The death of Clarence's wife Isabel at the end of 1476, shortly followed by Edward's brother-in-law Charles the Bold on 5 January 1477, set in motion a sequence of events that led to Clarence's destruction. Charles's death, with no male heir, put the whole future of the Burgundian state in jeopardy. Louis XI of France immediately took possession of Artois, Picardy and Burgundy itself. Charles's widow, Edward's sister Margaret, hastily proposed a marriage alliance between their brother Clarence and her stepdaughter Mary; the potential commercial benefits to England were huge. But this golden opportunity to achieve a dynastic link went begging.[29] Some councillors, including Edward's chamberlain Lord Hastings and possibly Richard of Gloucester, proposed armed intervention in support of the new duchess but were overruled.[30] Edward vetoed the marriage, partly because it would have torn up the treaty with France and the benefits he derived from it, partly because he would have had to support Clarence militarily, and because he still distrusted Clarence and feared his power should he become Duke of Burgundy. Rumours still circulated around the courts of Europe that Clarence was only waiting for the chance to make himself King of England.[31] Edward added insult to injury by proposing instead his brother-in-law, the queen's brother Anthony Woodville, Earl Rivers, also a widower.

Clarence was incandescent.[32] He made matters worse for himself by arresting, and summarily trying and condemning before the justices of the peace at Warwick, his late wife's lady-in-waiting, Ankaret Twynhoe, on a charge of poisoning her mistress. Twynhoe was executed the same day, along with another servant, John Thursby. It is possible that Thursby was a spy in Clarence's household passing information to the king, for it was said that both brothers were regularly receiving reports of what the other was saying.

By taking the law into his own hands, however, Clarence directly challenged the king's authority. Edward retaliated by arresting the prominent Oxford astrologer John Stacy, who confessed under torture that he had cast horoscopes on Clarence's behalf predicting the death of both the king and his son and heir Edward, Prince of Wales. Stacy and an associate, Thomas Burdet, a retainer of Clarence's, were found guilty and executed on 20 May. But the duke would not leave it there. He confronted the royal council with a declaration of the condemned men's innocence, read by Dr William Goddard, who had expounded Henry VI's title to the throne at his Readeption. The king could not fail to note the implicit threat and let this challenge to his authority pass. Towards the end of June Clarence was arrested and committed to the Tower on the charge of violating the laws of the realm.

There he lingered as the king and council thought long and hard before bringing him to trial. Sensationally, they decided to make it a charge of treason, and committed Clarence to be tried by his peers in a parliament called expressly and only for that purpose, which met in January 1478. The parliament was packed with the king's friends and the indictment, when it was finally crafted, was that the duke, notwithstanding the king's forbearance, had been both ungrateful and incorrigible: he had secured copies of letters of his nomination as heir to the throne in 1470 when he had rebelled against Edward; he had revived the rumours of Edward's illegitimacy that had been circulating in the late 1460s; he had encouraged Thomas Burdet to raise a rebellion; and in trying, condemning and executing Ankaret Twynhoe had usurped royal authority. Probably only the last charge could be proved and this, bad as it was, was not treason.

But Clarence had been arrogant and insubordinate. In his punishment of Ankaret Twynhoe he had taken the law into his own hands (even though many other powerful magnates had similarly erred without censure). Consulting astrologers was commonplace: Edward himself did so. Forecasting the king's death, if true, was a dangerous act. This was the charge that had undone Eleanor Cobham, Duchess of Gloucester in 1443. Publicly confronting and challenging the king in council was foolish; keeping a copy of his nomination as heir to the throne unwise. Edward was no doubt exasperated by Clarence; it is possible that despite their reconciliation in 1471, he always suspected him.

Notwithstanding the lack of evidence, Edward's parliament did as required: the House of Commons appealed Clarence and the House of Lords condemned him. Not a voice other than the king's, the Crowland chronicler reported, spoke against him; not a voice other than Clarence's own spoke in his defence.[33] It was a show trial. Sentence was passed on 7 February 1478. The king hesitated for ten days before signing the death warrant. On 20 February the duke was killed in the Tower privately and by means unknown, though rumours were soon circulating that he had been drowned in a butt of wine. His body was taken to Tewkesbury and buried there beside his duchess. Clarence was twenty-eight when he died, a young man of restless ambition, wayward talent and popular appeal, but blessed with little political judgement.[34]

Rumours that others, especially the queen and her family, had turned Edward against his brother cannot be discounted. He may well have been advised in late 1477 that he would have no peace unless he finally rid himself of Clarence. Their youngest brother, Richard of Gloucester, who might have intervened, apparently did not. His relationship with Clarence had been tense and he benefited from his fall. Sir Thomas More, many years later, went as far as to report that Richard 'lacked not in helping forth his brother Clarence to his death', which is so beautifully put that it ought to be true for that reason alone.[35] Just five years later Dominic Mancini, visiting London, heard that Richard blamed the queen's relations for Clarence's death, and vowed to revenge himself one day; but this story, circulating around the time he made himself king, is no more reliable.[36] All we can say with certainty is that Richard stood aside. In the last resort Edward, and Edward alone, destroyed his brother. Nothing can hide the fact that his execution was a shocking act of fratricide and the apparent settling of a personal score.

7
In Fear of No One

The Crowland chronicler, as an apologist for Edward, was deeply embarrassed by the whole Clarence affair, but he also noted that afterwards Edward was 'fully persuaded that he could rule as he pleased throughout the whole kingdom'. While he privately repented, he 'exercised his office so high-handedly thereafter, that he appeared to be feared by all his subjects while he himself stood in fear of no one'.[1] It is the case that for the remaining five years of his reign, with the fate of someone as mighty and close to the throne as the Duke of Clarence remembered by all his subjects, no one dared challenge him. He indeed ruled much as he pleased.

How did he please? Edward continued to rule through a small coterie of family members and his closest household servants. The destruction of Clarence led to a reordering of responsibilities in the east Midlands and West Country. The king's stepson, the Marquess of Dorset, might have stepped into Clarence's shoes for he was granted the wardship and right to arrange the marriage of Clarence's young son Edward, Earl of Salisbury (later Warwick), custody of some of his estates and a string of stewardships.[2] However, much of the Warwick inheritance was kept in royal hands and royal power was entrusted to local lords and household men such as Lord Dinham, who had proved their loyalty to Edward over the years. Dorset was to spend more time at court than in the provinces.

The role of the prince's council in Wales was strengthened so as to give it complete power over the principality, the earldom of March and other lordships in Wales in the king's hands. The chief beneficiary was Earl Rivers, the prince's governor, who was able to enhance considerably his authority and military power through the sweeping responsibility granted to the council in the prince's name.[3]

Richard of Gloucester consolidated his hold on the north of England after Clarence's fall, effectively ruling the region in the king's name. After 1478 he was indispensable to his brother, who could only acquiesce as his power increased. But he now kept his distance from the court. His continuing favour, however, as well as his growing authority in the north, was confirmed early in 1483 when Cumberland, including the wardenship of the West March, was created an hereditary palatinate for him.[4]

Closer to Westminster the king's rule was more direct, but in the east Midlands and East Anglia he began to create a patrimony for his second son, Richard of Shrewsbury, Duke of York. Its core was Fotheringhay, to which endowment Edward planned to add the duchy of Lancaster and York estates in the region. On the day before the opening of the parliament that condemned Clarence in January 1478, the five-year-old Richard was married with much splendour to Anne Mowbray, the child heiress of John, Duke of Norfolk, who had died in 1476. The

Mowbray estates were settled on the couple. A council playing a prominent role, similar to that originally established for the Prince of Wales, was constituted to administer the children's extensive interests.[5]

In these last years Edward became more dependent on a select group of kinsmen and senior household officers. They were supported locally by the knights and esquires of his body, an elite group granted the king's livery collar of suns and roses, who divided their time between serving at court and representing the crown in the provinces. The principal objective was to hold the realm steady and secure. As the Crowland chronicler observed, the king knew via his servants placed throughout the kingdom if any treason were plotted.[6] The regime remained markedly the rule of the victorious faction in a civil war. Edward made few attempts to reconcile the whole kingdom and all the great nobles to his regime. Henry Stafford, Duke of Buckingham, one of the greatest in the realm, was almost completely sidelined. He had extensive estates in Wales, the Midlands and Kent, but was given no government role or rewards, even though he was married to one of the queen's sisters.[7]

After 1478, then, Edward's regime became narrower and more partisan. Later, the Crowland chronicler remembered how 'many men' deserted him (by which he meant distanced themselves from his regime) after the death of Clarence.[8] Even within the inner circle there were resentments, enmities and rivalries that only the king's personal authority and charm could keep in check. There was considerable ill-feeling between Lord Hastings, Edward's chamberlain, and the Marquess of Dorset, while Hastings and the queen's brother Earl Rivers competed over the captaincy of Calais. Tensions also occurred between knights and esquires of the body, on whom everywhere Edward relied: in 1477 a bloody feud between two of his knights of the body, Sir John Saville and Sir John Pilkington, for domination of the royal lordship of Wakefield was only suppressed by a powerful special judicial commission of oyer and terminer under Richard of Gloucester.[9]

Few of Edward's subjects would have been aware of the rifts and tensions at court. They looked for good governance, by which they understood the maintenance of civil order, the fair and effective administration of the law and the promotion of prosperity. The main interaction between king and subject was in the receipt of and response to petitions on an almost daily basis. Edward issued many warrants signed by him with his own initials, 'RE' ('Rex Edwardus'). During these last years the signet consolidated its role as the dynamic administrative office of the crown, and the king's secretary as his most trusted administrator. Letters were sent from the king under the authority of his signet both to the principal offices of state (Chancery and Privy Seal), as well as directly to subjects. The Chamber, into which the French pension was paid, managed Edward's finances. Household government, as it has come to be styled, was initially a response to civil war, but it became permanent because of its direct answerability to the king and the speed with which action could be taken.[10]

While Edward continued to intervene in even relatively trivial cases, as when in 1479 he called Lord Cobham and his stepfather John Palmer before him to settle a quarrel,[11] the general level of disorder remained a matter of complaint by his subjects, resurfacing in 1483. The council of the duchy of Lancaster warned of continuing unrest in the county palatine in 1482. Concern about the extent of lawlessness was unabated.[12] Edward took what steps he could to improve the supervision of the law in the regions. The council in Wales was given a supervisory role in the administration of justice and held emergency powers in the border counties, including Shropshire. This supervisory role, through a permanent commission of oyer and terminer, was designed specifically to deal with any disorder caused by the Welsh. The council's records have not survived, so it is impossible to say how effective it was, but it marked a significant extension of central government into the administration of both the principality and the Marches.[13]

Richard of Gloucester intervened with the local authorities and justices of the peace in the north to speed the law, even on occasion against the interests of his own men. His council acted as an arbitration panel to which many appealed for the resolution of disputes. Through this, it was reported in 1483, he won the favour of the people in the north.[14] On the other hand Clarence, as we have seen, did not hesitate to pervert the course of justice in his own interest; others no doubt did so more subtly.[15] Perhaps Richard of Gloucester's high reputation was acquired because he was exceptional. All in all there was not a great improvement in the administration of justice even when Edward was totally secure on the throne. Ultimately the fair and effective administration of justice was subordinated to the political imperative of securing the regime and maintaining stability.[16]

Edward's personal imprint on government is plain to see. However, the line between a king making decisions and his delegating the formulation as well as implementation of policy to the council is sometimes hard to determine. There is no doubt that Henry V determined royal policy and that Henry VII imposed his authority on all. Edward IV was not as diligent or controlling as either Henry V or Henry VII; in modern parlance, he was more laid-back than either. He may have relied upon his council to develop and formulate policy rather more than had Henry V. But he chose talented and diligent administrators and councillors. The principal officers of state in his last years – Thomas Rotherham, Archbishop of York, as Chancellor from 1475; Henry Bourchier, Earl of Essex, as Treasurer; John Russell, Bishop of Lincoln, as the Keeper of the Privy Seal and John Morton, Bishop of Ely, ranking second in the Chancery as Master of the Rolls – formed an impressive team which oversaw the routine government of the realm.[17]

Chief Justice Sir John Fortescue, who entered the king's service after 1471, had written in exile a memorandum of advice for the young Lancastrian Prince of Wales on how he might, once he became king, reform the government of the realm. Central to his thinking was the notion that the crown must make itself considerably more mighty than any of its subjects; his diagnosis of the reason for the failure of Henry VI was the unconstrained power of subjects who were over-mighty and overbearing, most recently

Richard of York and the Earl of Warwick. There were two complementary elements to his proposed 'new foundation of his crown': one was to cut over-mighty subjects down to size; the other to increase the power and wealth of the crown by an inalienable endowment. Moreover he proposed that the royal council be more formally constituted as the executive of the crown, to a degree separated institutionally from the person of the monarch – something akin to Cabinet government. Elements of this programme of reform have been discerned in innovations later introduced by Henry VII: Edward IV has been credited with initiating a 'New Monarchy' along these lines.[18]

To some extent the problem of the over-mighty subject had resolved itself. In 1461 one of them, the Duke of York (Edward himself), had become king and his inheritance absorbed into the royal estate. The destruction of the Earl of Warwick and the division of his inheritance in 1471 removed another; while Richard of Gloucester was able to consolidate his hold on his half, Clarence had not been able to do so. After 1478 Edward took possession of the Beauchamp and Montagu lands in the southern counties, but only until Clarence's heir, Edward, Earl of Warwick, came of age. Moreover, the reward and promotion of his immediate family towards the end of his reign and the creation of a palatinate in the far north-west for his surviving brother suggests that Edward was in the process of promoting new mighty subjects. At the same time, enhancement of the crown estate through forfeiture and resumption was often of secondary importance to the distribution of rewards for short-term political ends.

Of equal concern to Edward and his councillors was what Fortescue characterized as the resentment of the common people at having to pay taxes to support an impoverished king.[19] It was a concern echoed in Crowland's view that the king amassed treasure towards the end of his reign so that there would be no need to tax his subjects and provoke disturbances.[20] Unrest had continued into the early 1460s, resurfaced in 1469–71 and flickered again in 1475–6.

It can be assumed that the young Edward, like his father, had always been uneasy with the Earl of Warwick's endorsement of the notion of popular sovereignty. Warwick himself did not for a moment believe it, but for political ends he gave it credence. After his overthrow, Edward and his advisers were determined to reassert the absolute, unlimited sovereignty of the crown. In 1486 the Crowland chronicler recalled with horror how the kingdom had been destabilized by 'idols of the multitude' – he was thinking primarily of Warwick – 'to whom the eyes of the common folk, ever eager for change, used to turn in times gone by'.[21] It was with the events of 1450–71 in mind that Bishop John Russell had planned to appeal to the Lords in the intended opening of the first parliament of Edward V's reign to maintain unity and not call on popular support. For, he declared, the people must stand afar. 'It suffices them to receive with due obeisance the king's commandments.'[22] The determination to restrict political participation to the privileged elites was part and parcel of the drive, continued under Edward's successors, to enhance the authority of the crown over all its subjects.

In the last resort, Chief Justice Fortescue argued, the crown would only assert its supreme authority over all its subjects if it were well endowed. Edward had declared to the parliament of 1468 that he intended to live of his own, to pay for all his regular expenditure from his own resources as king. This he at first failed to do. At his disposal he had the income of customs and excise, granted to him for life by parliament in 1465, and the revenue from the crown's landed estate; benefiting too from a general upturn in rental income, the yield was increased. On top of this after 1475 he received the French pension of £10,000 a year. Edward also enjoyed a rise in customs revenue, from some £24,000 a year early in his reign to £34,000 towards its end. This was generated in part by a tightening of administration but mainly by the revival of trade after 1471, especially in woollen cloths exported to the Burgundian Netherlands. Not only did England recover from the deep recession of the previous two decades, but merchants also prospered from commercial treaties negotiated in 1467 and 1478. Some savings were also made: annuities were curtailed and the running costs of the royal household trimmed. By the end of the reign annual income from regular sources, excluding taxation and benevolences, had risen to some £65,000–70,000 compared to £50,000 in 1461.[23]

It was asserted even before his death, and has been alleged since, that Edward was avaricious and his judgement clouded by his greed. This even appears in one of the laments for the dead king written in 1483, in which his soul is imagined to be recalling his life and asking for prayers to be said on his behalf. In one stanza he remembers

> I stored my coffers and also my chests
> With taxes taken of the commonalty;
> I took their treasure, but of their prayers mist
> Whom I beseech with pure humility
> For to forgive and have on me pity[24]

Behind a conventional plea to God to pardon the financial improprieties of the deceased lies a widespread contemporary perception of him over-taxing his subjects. First appearing in Warkworth's chronicle written before his death, it was picked up by Mancini and repeated by the Crowland chronicler, who was particularly incensed at Edward's taxation of the clergy.[25] He profited significantly from the devaluation of the coinage in 1464–5 and engaged privately in lucrative trading ventures throughout his reign. The recourse in 1480 to a further benevolence, without parliamentary authority, even more successfully than in 1474, aroused considerable resentment, adding to this image of a rapacious monarch. Knowing the names and circumstances of all the men of substance throughout the kingdom, which the Crowland chronicler found remarkable, would have been helpful in tapping them for a loving gift.[26] However, while it is clear that he did not waste any opportunity for profit, it is not easy to draw the line between personal greed and royal policy.

To the charge of avarice, a conventional criticism of an overbearing king, was added the belief that he did indeed hoard his revenue and that he died, unusually for a medieval king, with a financial surplus and a great treasure stashed away. While it is true that Edward sought every opportunity to increase his revenue, he also spent heavily not only on his magnificent court and lifestyle, but also in his last years on his campaigns against the Scots. Moreover, after his death it was discovered that the supposed hoard was a myth.[27] Nevertheless he had restored royal finances to a sound basis and successfully created the illusion of being wealthy.[28] This in itself was a significant achievement.

Edward was not, however, interested in long-term reform. While his council may have promoted Fortescue's ideas, his interest in them extended no further than how they might give him more money to spend and keep him secure on the throne. Permanent endowment of the crown, let alone institutionalized conciliar government, was unthinkable. Any revival of royal authority along the lines similar to those recommended by Fortescue was fortuitous. The widening of the gap between the power of the crown and of mighty subjects happened as much in spite of as because of Edward IV's intentions. Only in the firm reassertion of absolute royal sovereignty over popular challenge did Edward IV fully anticipate policies that were to be pursued by Henry VII after 1485.

Philippe de Commynes was in no doubt that Edward's foreign policy in his last years was determined solely by greed, in particular an obsession to retain at all costs his pension from Louis XI.[29] In August 1477, after Edward had rejected the match between the Duke of Clarence and Mary of Burgundy and refused to back her cause with armed intervention, Mary had married the eighteen-year-old Maximilian Habsburg, Archduke of Austria, who immediately came to the defence of her lands in the Low Countries. Edward endeavoured to maintain a delicate balance between France and Burgundy, trying both to ensure the survival of the Burgundian state and to retain the benefits of the Treaty of Picquigny of 1475, the proposed marriage between his first-born daughter Elizabeth and Louis XI's heir, as well as the pension. The traditional policy of a Burgundian alliance for commercial ends was pitched against the king's financial and family interests deriving from the treaty. In adopting a position of neutrality in the war between Burgundy and France Edward embarked on a tortuous game, playing one side against the other for his support. Maximilian was keen to recover territories lost before his marriage and to reconstruct the triple alliance of England, Brittany and Burgundy against Louis XI which had collapsed in 1475. Edward used the potential threat of military support for Maximilian to secure continued payments of his pension from Louis XI and to press for the confirmation of the marriage of his daughter Elizabeth to the Dauphin.[30]

However, after Maximilian won a decisive victory at Guinegate near Thérouanne in Artois in August 1479, Edward leaned towards a Burgundian alliance. Margaret, dowager Duchess of Burgundy (the king's sister), who was received lavishly on a state visit to England in July 1480, acted as an intermediary in a treaty sealed with Maximilian in August that year in which his infant son Philip, the heir to the duchy of Burgundy, would marry Edward's daughter Anne and Maximilian agreed to take over the pension. Not surprisingly, Louis XI suspended payment. Edward also opened negotiations with the Duke of Brittany for the renewal of their alliance, through a marriage between the Prince of Wales and the duke's heir Anne. A new triple alliance against Louis XI was beginning to take shape.

By this time Edward was also drawn into conflict with Scotland. The peace treaty of 1474 between the two kingdoms came under strain in 1479 with the outbreak of cross-border raiding. The Crowland chronicler believed that Louis XI's hand was somewhere in this, encouraging King James III of Scotland.[31] Tit-for-tat raiding intensified in 1480, with Richard of Gloucester taking the lead on the English side as the king's lieutenant. In 1481 Edward decided to mount a full-scale invasion of Scotland, even as he was negotiating a treaty of mutual aid with Brittany. Drawing upon the last instalment of the subsidy raised in 1475 but not collected, and a new round of benevolences, he mobilized an army with the intention of leading it himself against the Scots. In the end he went no further than Nottingham, leaving it to continue north under Richard, under whom it threatened Berwick and raided across the border, but otherwise achieved nothing.

Edward persisted, rejecting pressure from Maximilian to honour their agreement by at least sending troops to his assistance. Instead he took advantage of the defection of James III's brother, Alexander, Duke of Albany, who fled to England in April 1482. At the Treaty of Fotheringhay on 11 June Edward recognized Alexander as King of Scots and agreed to assist him in securing the throne in return for the cession of Berwick and a significant stretch of south-west Scotland. The military command was entrusted to Richard of Gloucester, who led a substantial army north. The town of Berwick fell quickly. Leaving a force to invest the castle, Gloucester marched unopposed to Edinburgh. Thereupon Albany made his peace with James III, and Gloucester had no choice but to return to England, completing the capture of Berwick Castle en route at the end of August.

It is hard to understand why Edward was diverted by war against Scotland. It soured his relationship with Maximilian. Edward delayed ratification of his treaty with him. At the same time he secretly assured Louis XI that he would not be party to a hostile alliance against France, in return for which in August Louis resumed payment of the pension. It has been suggested that Edward was attracted by the prospect of an easy victory on his northern border and that he saw the recapture of Berwick, surrendered by Margaret of Anjou in 1461, as completing his recovery of his kingdom. On the other hand, Edward may have been pushed in this direction by his brother Richard. Border raiding was popular in the north. Richard of Gloucester had taken an independently aggressive line against Scotland before 1474 and had only reluctantly accepted the Treaty of Edinburgh, which established peace between the two kingdoms on the eve of the king's expedition to France. After the death of Clarence Edward was dangerously dependent on his younger brother and could not afford to alienate him, thereby threatening once more the internal peace of the kingdom.

8
The End of Summer

Edward's continental policy fell apart in 1482. In March Mary, the young Duchess of Burgundy, died after a riding accident, leaving her son Philip as the child duke. Maximilian attempted but failed to have himself installed as regent. The representative assembly of Flanders, which controlled the ducal purse strings, defied him and assumed the regency for itself, asserting control over foreign policy. Its members had grown increasingly opposed to Maximilian's war, which they had been financing. In the name of their young duke they opened negotiations with Louis XI, who published his secret agreement with Edward IV of the previous year. Maximilian had little choice but to enter into negotiation with Louis to end the war, and by the Treaty of Arras on 23 December 1482 he agreed the marriage of the Dauphin to his daughter Margaret, Philip's sister, with Artois, Picardy and Burgundy, already in French hands, as her dowry. Louis promptly suspended payment of his pension to Edward.

Edward had been outmanoeuvred and left isolated. He lost all he had gained at Picquigny. His foreign policy was in tatters. There was nothing unusual in endeavouring to play Burgundy against France to his own advantage. But he may have been too clever by half. Certainly the Scottish campaigns made matters more complex. On the other hand, he might simply have been unlucky, for he could not have anticipated the death of Mary of Burgundy and its consequences.

Edward was furious. Although at first said to be delighted at the recovery of Berwick, later he grumbled at its cost and pointlessness.[1] His anger at what he saw as Louis XI's betrayal was such, it was rumoured, that he could talk of nothing else but revenging himself on France. A parliament had been summoned on 15 November, before the Treaty of Arras, to meet at Westminster on 20 January 1483, at which a subsidy for the hasty and necessary defence of the realm was also voted. If not against France, it might have been for renewal of the war against Scotland. Albany, the English-backed pretender to the Scottish throne, had once more fled to England and the Treaty of Fotheringhay, by which Edward agreed to place Albany on the throne, was confirmed on 12 February 1483, six days before parliament was dissolved. In addition several acts were passed manipulating inheritances for the benefit of the king's son, the young Richard, Duke of York and his stepson Thomas, Marquess of Dorset, as well as creating the palatinate in the far north-west for Richard of Gloucester. It may be significant that the act benefiting Gloucester granted to him those lands ceded at Fotheringhay and which the duke, in the wording of the statute, undertook to conquer. Gloucester's influence seems in no way to have been harmed by the disastrous outcome of the king's foreign policy.[2]

More questionable were the acts benefiting his stepsons and own second son. The inheritance of the late Duke of Exeter, he who had fallen overboard in 1475, was settled on Elizabeth Woodville's sons by her first marriage, the Marquess of Dorset and his brother Sir Richard Grey. This was done at the expense of the expectations of Ralph, Lord Neville, one of Richard of Gloucester's closest associates and the late duke's nearest male heir. A second act, following two years after the death of his child bride Anne Mowbray (the Norfolk heir), made young Richard, Duke of York the heir to the whole duchy of Norfolk. Lord Howard, a man who had loyally and effectively served the king since the beginning of the reign, was one of the residual heirs to the duchy. Howard might have expected to come into his share of this inheritance. Edward put the endowment of his own family before both the laws of inheritance and the expectations of one his most loyal servants.[3]

By now Edward's hedonistic lifestyle and 'over-liberal diet' were taking their toll. He was obese. He had, Mancini remarked shortly after his death, grown 'fat in the loins', or as More put it more kindly, 'somewhat corpulent and burly', or Commynes more bluntly: 'very fat and gross'.[4] Gone were the days when he could caper nimbly in a lady's chamber: it was not surprising, as Thomas More heard, that his 'fleshly wantonness' was abated. The once handsome man was by his last year a sad ruin of his former self. Yet he still kept up appearances. Londoners remembered how he entertained several prominent citizens at a great hunt in Waltham Forest in the autumn of 1482. At

Christmas that year he appeared in many different gowns, all in the latest continental fashion.[5]

Not long after the end of the parliament, late in March 1483, Edward became seriously ill. Accounts vary over the nature of his illness. It has been suggested that it was induced by depression, that he caught a cold while out on a fishing party, that he was poisoned or, the most frequently cited, that it was the result of a stroke, linked to his lifestyle and obesity. This is the most likely; though if so, he was still able to think and speak lucidly until his death two or three weeks later.[6] But he was gravely ill, for a report reached York on 6 April that he was already dead. In fact he lingered on for three more days.

Edward added codicils to his will on his deathbed, though the details have not survived.[7] In his last days the king sought to reconcile at least two of his rival courtiers: the Marquess of Dorset and Lord Hastings.[8] No other attempted reconciliation was recorded. Historians for long believed that similar intense rivalry existed between Earl Rivers and Richard of Gloucester. If so – and there is evidence to suggest that the two were working amicably together shortly before the king's death – no personal reconciliation could be attempted because neither was at court: Rivers was at Ludlow and Gloucester in north Yorkshire. Gloucester later claimed that Edward had set down in one of the missing codicils that he wished him to be the protector of the kingdom and the king's young sons to be placed in his care. This may have been so. But the precedent had been established following the death of Henry V in 1422 that a king could not rule beyond the grave and the

last wishes of a monarch for the government of the kingdom during a minority held no force in law.

The Crowland chronicler was content that Edward,
having made all the necessary provisions, had a good
death – indeed, for such a worldly prince the best of all
possible ends, especially, he noted, for one who had
indulged too intemperately in his own passions. He made
full and proper atonement for his sins before he gave up his
soul to his Maker.[9] Edward's body was laid out in the palace at Westminster for a day before being embalmed,
placed in a coffin and moved to St Stephen's Chapel, where
it lay for eight days while vigil was kept and Masses sung
for his soul. The funeral was set for Windsor on 19 April.[10]

It is puzzling that no effort seems to have been made to
escort the new king, Edward V, from Ludlow to attend the
funeral. He did not in fact set out until after his father's
burial. Likewise the king's brother did not leave Yorkshire
until later in the month. It has been suggested that the
council in London, which was making the arrangements
for the funeral and the government of the realm during the
minority, made sure that they completed the obsequies
before they could arrive. But there was no unseemly haste.
It may have been that, for reasons not now known, neither
Earl Rivers nor Richard of Gloucester chose to hurry down
to Westminster.

Those who had been at hand when the king died made
the arrangements for the funeral. They included the senior
officers of the household, Lords Hastings and Stanley and
Sir William Parr; other councillors, among them Archbishop Rotherham of York, John Morton, Bishop of Ely

and John Russell, Bishop of Lincoln, as well as the queen, her son the Marquess of Dorset and her younger brother, Edward. The last rites were conducted with all the pomp and ceremony expected of a royal funeral. The coffin was first moved in procession to Westminster Abbey, where it was placed in a specially constructed hearse. The cortège then set out for Windsor via Syon Abbey, where it rested on the night of 17 April. The procession travelled from there to Windsor on the following day, and the coffin was placed in St George's Chapel overnight.

The funeral and burial on 19 April were attended by the majority of the peers, many senior clergy, a considerable number of the king's knights and esquires of the body and all the heralds, crammed into the half-completed chapel. As was customary, the achievements (arms and banners) of the king were offered. At the end of the ceremony the senior officers of the household, who had played a prominent role in the proceedings, cast their broken staves of office into the open grave.[11] Edward was buried 'low in the ground', under the ground floor, or vault, of his two-storey chantry chapel which was under contruction. It would seem that he requested a 'transi' tomb – a figure of himself as a cadaver below, a representation of him in full silver and gilt armour above – in the chapel. His queen was laid to rest above him in 1492. But his effigy was never executed. All that marked the spot were his achievements, which were hung above the grave after the funeral and which survived until 1642. The burial vault was rediscovered in 1789. When the coffin was opened the corpse was found to be preserved, though it rapidly turned to dust on exposure to the air.[12] The rebuilt chapel itself remains the principal memorial to him.

Edward IV's funeral was an impressively orchestrated piece of theatre designed to demonstrate the unity in which he had left his kingdom and the great love that his subjects had had for him. Four laments for the dead king circulated shortly after his death, all dwelling on the transitoriness of life, exhorting prayers for his soul and extolling his achievements. They seem to have been composed by members of his entourage. One, 'The Death of Edward IV', imagines him still alive in his magnificent court moving among his lords and knights, all of whom are now desolate that he is 'past and gone'. He was simply without comparison, no other prince could match him; he was the 'well of knighthood without peer'. He even conquered France 'without stroke'. All England will join in praying for his soul.[13] There is much that is conventional in these verses, but they seem to reflect the genuine grief of his household at his sudden passing. The authors would not have foreseen that their world was about to collapse and that England would within a matter of weeks be plunged into turmoil again and that his tomb would never be completed.

Two months later, Edward IV was followed to the grave by Louis XI. The new King of France, Charles VIII, was a minor and, had Edward lived, the chance may have presented itself for a revival of the triple alliance against France which Edward and Maximilian had been planning in 1481. Indeed this opportunity arose when Maximilian recovered his control over Flanders in 1485. As it was,

Edward's death two weeks before his forty-first birthday left England itself with a minority and, in the crises that rapidly followed, unable to take advantage.

The new King of England, Edward V, was twelve years old; his younger brother Richard not yet ten. Within three months of his accession Edward V was deposed by his uncle, Richard of Gloucester. One theme that echoes through all accounts of the remarkable course of events is that everyone trusted Richard of Gloucester, the dead king's loyal brother, the one man they believed who could be relied upon to ensure that the young king would reach his majority and in time take up the reins of government. In fact Gloucester acted decisively and ruthlessly, wrongfooting all opposition, to secure for himself by force first the government of the kingdom and control of the person of the king and then, six weeks later, the throne itself. Several who stood in his way were summarily executed, including Earl Rivers and Lord Hastings. It cannot be demonstrated that he also ordered the deaths of the boy king and his younger brother before or shortly after he was crowned. Nevertheless they disappeared.[14]

The rights and wrongs of Richard III's coup d'état have been endlessly debated. He may have acted in self-defence against plots to destroy him emanating from the new queen mother and her family. He may, or may not, have discovered that his nephews, or even his brother, were illegitimate. He may have calculated that his long-term prospects under an adult rule of Edward V were not good and that it would be safer to hazard the seizure of the throne. He may have stumbled more by accident than design from one step to another that led to his accession. Or he may have been a deep dissembler and hypocrite, as Mancini at the time came to believe and Shakespeare elaborated, who saw and seized his chance to secure the ultimate prize.[15]

It is conventional to cite the biblical text 'woe to thee, O land, when thy king is a child'[16] when considering the troubles that accompany minorities and in particular the fate of the princes. But England had – albeit with difficulty – weathered other such minorities. Both Richard II and Henry VI came of age and took over the rule of their kingdoms: Henry VI, indeed, had done so after sixteen years of a royal minority. No other minority in English history was terminated violently, within three months, in the way that Edward V's reign was.

Why was Edward IV's immediate legacy so short-lived? Traditionally the blame is placed on the shoulders of the treacherous Richard III, whose betrayal of his trust could not have been foreseen.[17] However, as we have noted, there were fault lines in the regime. Rivalries at court were kept in check only by the king's personal authority. A small but significant number of excluded and embittered lords resented their treatment at the dead king's hands. The excluded Henry Stafford, Duke of Buckingham, and the slighted John, Lord Howard, quickly created Duke of Norfolk, were early adherents of Richard III. There were undercurrents of dissatisfaction about the manner in which the kingdom had apparently been ruled for the benefit of a favoured few, especially the queen's relations.

Fundamentally Edward's regime had remained to the very end the narrow rule of a victorious faction in civil war. Too much power in the provinces had been given to too few great lords personally close to the king. Only half-hearted attempts had been made to unite the whole kingdom behind the dynasty. Edward had not healed dynastic division on the fields of France, as Henry V had so notably done.[18] Had he too won great victories over the French his dynasty might have flourished; by the same token it probably would not have survived defeat. Whether or not this was the critical factor, Edward's failure to create a collective commitment to his dynasty under his son explains how Richard of Gloucester, with the benefit of complete surprise, was able to seize the throne.

Edward's was a sadly dysfunctional family. Both his brothers betrayed him; in exasperated revenge he judicially murdered the elder; the younger without provocation in turn destroyed his children. Crowland recalled that the brothers possessed such talents that, had they been able to avoid discord, such a triple bond could only have been broken with the utmost difficulty.[19] Surely he was right. Edward was also estranged from his mother after his marriage in 1464. She was later rumoured to have disowned him, while she had apparently supported the plan to depose him in favour of Clarence in 1470. She and her eldest son made their peace in 1471, but thereafter she rarely came to court other than to attend family events.[20] Edward seems to have been closest to his sister Margaret, Duchess of Burgundy. Yorkist disharmony stands in contrast to the bond between Henry V and his brothers, and the evident commitment of the two surviving brothers to his infant heir, Henry VI, after his death in 1422.

Given Edward's untimely death and the tragic events that swiftly followed, what was his achievement? His priority after 1471 was to stay on the throne and enjoy the fruits of victory. Like Charles II two centuries later, he would not, as the Stuart monarch was wont to declare, go on his travels again. In this he succeeded. Edward ruled effectively enough to bring an end in his own lifetime to the civil wars that brought him to the throne. He inspired the loyalty of his closest servants, if not of his brothers. He was a man of considerable charm, who perhaps relied too much upon that charm to keep tensions within his entourage at bay. He was a great warrior who preferred not to fight, one who by temperament was a knight of Venus rather than of Mars. He was capable of great energy and decisiveness in a crisis, yet could be indolent and self-indulgent when all seemed well. He enjoyed the 'lascivious pleasing of a lute' in his bedchamber, yet cast a watchful eye on the money passing through his financial Chamber. Often merciful and conciliatory to his enemies, he could be casually brutal and vengeful. While proclaiming his commitment to the law, he did not hesitate to bend it for the benefit of his family or override it to dispose of his rivals.

In many ways his grandson, Henry VIII, took after him: he too was a tall, handsome young man, with the same narrow eyes and pinched mouth. Both went spectacularly to fat; both shared an enthusiasm for jousting and the hunt. Edward was a successful general who preferred not to fight; Henry wanted to fight but lacked his grandfather's talent. Edward was a sexual predator in a way that Henry, for all the misplaced titillation about his six wives, never was. On the other hand, Edward never inspired the same dread or fear as his grandson. Henry, too, oversaw a major change in the direction taken by the kingdom; Edward IV made no such impact.

Had he lived longer and successfully established his dynasty Edward, rather than Henry VII, would probably be remembered as the man who restored peace, prosperity and stability to an England torn apart by civil war. In so far as he governed more directly through his household, improved royal finances and reasserted the authority of the crown over his subjects, he began a process that continued under the early Tudors. He himself had no grand vision of that end. Perhaps his councillors and servants thought in longer terms about the monarchy: many continued to serve under Henry VII. A direct line of civil servants administering the realm in the interests of the crown irrespective of the person of the king can be traced from John Morton to Thomas Cromwell. They, as much as any individual king, shaped the institutional structure of the early modern monarchy.[21]

Edward IV himself did not look much beyond his immediate personal interests and desires. The promise and hopes of his supporters for a new beginning soon evaporated. He proved, despite his undoubted charm, to be a man of fitful energy, limited vision and short-term aspiration. His failure to hand his throne on to his son is damning. But even so there was an element of ill-luck in Edward's early death. Fortune's wheel turned too soon for the house of York. Had Edward lived a further four years, it is unlikely that Richard III's usurpation would have been possible. Henry VII, who had been at death's door several times, hung on until 1509 when his heir was seventeen and able to succeed without a risky minority. For Edward IV, tragically, summer's lease had all too short a span.

Abbreviations

Arrivall of Edward IV	*Historie of the Arrivall of Edward IV*, ed. J. Bruce (London: Camden Society, 1838)
Commynes, *Memoirs*	Philippe de Commynes, *Memoirs: The Reign of Louis XI*, trans. Michael Jones (Harmondsworth: Penguin, 1972)
Crowland Chronicle Continuations	*The Crowland Chronicle Continuations, 1459–86*, ed. N. Pronay and J. C. Cox (Gloucester: Alan Sutton, 1986)
Davis, *Paston Letters*	*Paston Letters and Papers of the Fifteenth Century*, ed. N. Davis et al., 3 vols (Oxford: Oxford University Press, 2004–5)
Gairdner, *Paston Letters*	*Paston Letters, 1422–1509*, ed. J. Gairdner, 6 vols (London: Chatto & Windus, 1904)
Great Chronicle	*The Great Chronicle of London*, ed. A. H. Thomas and I. D. Thornley (London: privately published, 1938)
Hicks, *Edward IV*	Michael Hicks, *Edward IV* (London: Arnold, Hodder Education, 2004)

Kleineke, *Edward IV*	Hannes Kleineke, *Edward IV* (Abingdon: Routledge, 2009)
Mancini, *Usurpation*	Dominic Mancini, *The Usurpation of Richard III*, ed. C. A. J. Armstrong, 2nd edn (Oxford: Clarendon Press, 1969)
More, *History*	St Thomas More, *The History of King Richard III and Selections for the English and Latin Poems*, ed. R. S. Sylvester (New Haven and London: Yale University Press, 1976)
PROME	*Parliament Rolls of Medieval England*, ed. C. Given-Wilson (Scholars Digital Editions, 2005)
Ross, *Edward IV*	Charles Ross, *Edward IV* (London: Eyre Methuen, 1974)
Rot Parl	*Rotuli Parliamentorum*, ed. J. Strachey et al., 6 vols (Westminster: House of Lords, 1767–77)
TNA	The National Archives
TRHS	*Transactions of the Royal Historical Society*
Warkworth, *Chronicle*	John Warkworth, *A Chronicle of the First Thirteen Years of the Reign of Edward IV*, ed. J. O. Halliwell (London: Camden Society, 1839)

Notes

1. A NOTABLE FOUNDATION OF HEARSAY

1. *Crowland Chronicle Continuations*, especially pp. 125–7, 137–9, 143, 147–51; Hicks, *Edward IV*, pp. 46–53. For recent discussion of the vexed question of the author's identity see Michael Hicks, 'The Second Anonymous Continuation of the Crowland Abbey Chronicle 1459–86 Revisited', *English Historical Review*, cxxii (2007), pp. 349–70 and Alison Hanham, 'The Mysterious Affair at Crowland Abbey', *The Ricardian*, xviii (2008), pp. 1–20.

2. Commynes, *Memoirs*, pp. 184, 188, 361, 413–14; Hicks, *Edward IV*, pp. 40–45.

3. Mancini, *Usurpation*, pp. 65–9; A. J. Pollard, 'Dominic Mancini's Narrative of the Events of 1483', *Nottingham Medieval Studies*, xxxviii (1994), pp. 152–63.

4. *Three Books of Polydore Vergil's English History*, ed. H. Ellis (London: Camden XXXIX, 1844), pp. 167–8, 172.

5. More, *History*, pp. 3–6, 70–76.

6. 'Gregory's Chronicle', in *Historical Collections of a Citizen of London*, ed. J. Gairdner (London: Camden, new series, XVII, 1876), pp. 58–239; *An English Chronicle, 1377–1461*, ed. W. Marx (Woodbridge: Boydell, 2003); C. L. Kingsford, *Chronicles of London* (Oxford: Oxford University Press, 1905); *Great Chronicle*.

7. *Chronicle of the Rebellion in Lincolnshire*, ed. J. G. Nichols (London: Camden, 1847); *Arrivall of Edward IV*.

8. Warkworth, *Chronicle*; *Death and Dissent: The Dethe of the King of Scots and Warkworth's Chronicle*, ed. L. Matheson (Woodbridge: Boydell, 1999).

9. M. A. Hicks, 'The Sources', in *The Wars of the Roses*, ed. A. J. Pollard (Basingstoke: Macmillan, 1995), pp. 20–40.

10. Sir Philip Sidney, *An Apology for Poetry*, ed. G. Shepherd (Manchester: Manchester University Press, 1973), p. 105.

11. J. R. Lander, 'Edward IV, The Modern Legend and a Revision', in *Crown and Nobility, 1450–1509* (London: Edward Arnold, 1976), pp. 160–62; Hicks, *Edward IV*, pp. 62–73.

12. William Stubbs, *A Constitutional History of England during the Middle Ages*, III (Oxford: Oxford University Press, 1898), pp. 236–7, 295; J. R. Green, *A Short History of the English People* (London: Macmillan, 1874), p. 286.

13. William Edwards, *Notes on British History* (London: Rivington, 5th edn 1958), p. 232. I'm grateful to Hugh Meller for this reference.

14. M. C. Carpenter, *The Wars of the Roses: Politics and the Constitution in England, c.1437–1509* (Cambridge: Cambridge University Press, 1997), pp. 180–205 following on Lander, 'Edward IV', pp. 169–70.

15. C. F. Richmond, '1485 and All That, or what was really going on at the Battle of Bosworth?', in *Richard III: Loyalty, Lordship and Law*, ed. P. W. Hammond (Richard III and Yorkist History Trust, 2nd edn 2000), pp. 226–36; C. F. Richmond and M. L. Kekewich, 'The Search for Stability, 1461–83', in *The Politics of Fifteenth-Century England*, ed. M. L. Kekewich et al. (Stroud: Alan Sutton, 1995), pp. 43–53, 67–72.

16. J. R. Green, *History of the English People*, II (London: Macmillan, 1878), pp. 27–8; idem, *Short History*, p. 286; J. Ashdown Hill, *Eleanor: The Secret Queen* (Stroud: The History Press, 2009), p. 133. However, as Lander pointed out, dissipation does not necessarily preclude application ('Edward IV', p. 169).

2. SON OF YORK

1. Commynes, *Memoirs*, p. 249.

2. M. K. Jones, *Bosworth 1485: Psychology of a Battle* (Stroud: Tempus 2002), pp. 65–71 makes the case for illegitimacy, based on the absence of York from Rouen in August 1441 when Edward would have been conceived. However, Jones overlooks evidence of York having returned there on 1 August in a break from campaigning in the Oise valley (A. J. Pollard, 'The Family of Talbot, Lords Talbot and Earls of Shrewsbury in the Fifteenth Century', University of Bristol PhD thesis, 1968), pp. 180–81.

3. Mancini, *Usurpation*, pp. 61–3.

4. Ibid., pp. 95–7.

5. *Rot Parl*, VI, p. 241.

6. For Edward's upbringing see Ross, *Edward IV*, pp. 7–9; Kleineke, *Edward IV*, pp. 28–34.

7. *Original Letters Illustrative of English History*, 1st series, ed. H. Ellis (London: Harding, Triphook and Lepard, 1824), pp. i, 9–10.

8. Kingsford, *Chronicles of London*, p. 163; Gairdner, *Paston Letters*, II, p. 297.

9. For the events of 1459–61 see Ross, *Edward IV*, pp. 20–38; Kleineke, *Edward IV*, pp. 34–47; R. A. Griffiths, *The Reign of Henry VI: The Exercise of Royal Authority* (London: Ernest Benn, 1981), pp. 817–82; A. J. Pollard, *Warwick the Kingmaker: Politics, Power and Fame* (London: Hambledon Continuum, 2007), pp. 39–51.

10. For this and the following paragraphs see J. L. Watts, 'The Pressure of the Public on Later Medieval Politics', in *The Fifteenth Century 4: Political Culture in Late Medieval Britain*, ed. L. S. Clark and M. C. Carpenter (Woodbridge: Boydell, 2004), pp. 159–80 and idem, 'Ideas, Principles and Politics', in *The Wars of the Roses*, ed. A. J. Pollard, pp. 110–33; Pollard, *Warwick the Kingmaker*, pp. 147–65 and idem, 'The People, Politics and the Constitution in the Fifteenth Century', in *Law, Governance and Justice: New Views on Medieval Constitutionalism*, ed. Richard W. Kaeuper (Leiden: Brill, 2013), pp. 311–30.

11. Gairdner, *Paston Letters*, III, p. 204; Davis, *Paston Letters*, I, no. 88.

12. Jonathan Hughes, *Arthurian Myths and Alchemy: The Kingship of Edward IV* (Stroud: Sutton, 2002), pp. 83–5.

13. The two were also combined as the rose en soleil.
14. *Historical Collections of London Citizen*, ed. Gairdner, p. 215.

3. THIS FAIR WHITE ROSE

1. Commynes, *Memoirs*, p. 413; Jean de Waurin, *Anchiennes Cronicques d'Engleterre*, ed. Mlle Dupont (Paris: Société de la Histoire de France, 1858–63), pp. iii, 184.
2. For the establishment of the regime see Ross, *Edward IV*, pp. 42–83; Kleineke, *Edward IV*, pp. 48–71.
3. Kleineke, *Edward IV*, pp. 57–60.
4. *Rot Parl*, V, p. 464; *PROME*, Edward IV, 1461, November, Texts/Translations, no. 3.10.
5. Hughes, *Arthurian Myths*, pp. 116–61, especially at pp. 133–5.
6. S. J. Payling, 'Edward IV and the Politics of Conciliation in the Early 1460s', in *The Yorkist Age*, ed. Hannes Kleineke and Christian Steer (Donington: Shaun Tyas, 2013), pp. 81–94.
7. James Ross, *John de Vere, Thirteenth Earl of Oxford, 1442–1513* (Woodbridge: Boydell, 2011), pp. 38–46; M. A. Hicks, 'Edward IV, the Duke of Somerset and Lancastrian Loyalism in the North', *Northern History*, 20 (1978). Somerset, killed at Hexham in 1464, was succeeded by his brother Edmund.
8. *An English Chronicle*, ed. Marx, p. 78.
9. Ibid., pp. 240–43; A. L. Brown, *The Governance of Medieval England, 1272–1461* (London: Edward Arnold, 1989), pp. 100–40; E. Powell, 'Law and Justice', in *Fifteenth-Century Attitudes*, ed. R. E. Horrox (Cambridge: Cambridge University Press, 1994), pp. 29–41.
10. For the bureaucracy inherited by Edward see Brown, *Governance of Medieval England*, passim.
11. His remains were disinterred in 1789 and his skeleton measured six feet three and a half inches. Anne F. Sutton and Livia Visser-Fuchs, *The Royal Funerals of the House of York at Windsor* (London: Richard III Society, 2005), p. 115.
12. *PROME*, Edward IV, 1461, November, Texts/Translations, no. 2.7; Commynes, *Memoirs*, p. 84.
13. Ross, *Edward IV*, pp. 8–9, Commynes, *Memoirs*, damned his French with faint praise as 'quite good', p. 258.
14. C. L. Scofield, *The Life and Reign of Edward the Fourth*, 2 vols (London: Longmans, Green and Co., 1923), I, p. 300; II appendix 1, pp. 461–2.
15. John Ashdown Hill, 'The Elusive Mistress: Elizabeth Lucy and her Family', *The Ricardian*, xi, 145 (1999), pp. 490–505. But see Hicks, *Edward IV*, pp. 35–7, who argues that she was Margaret Lucy, widow of Sir William Lucy killed at Northampton, who herself died on 4 August 1466.
16. John Ashdown Hill, *Eleanor: The Secret Queen* (Stroud: The History Press, 2009), pp. 102–10.
17. Kleineke, *Edward IV*, p. 79, citing TNA E101/411/15, fo. 14v.
18. Mancini, *Usurpation*, p. 61.
19. Ashdown Hill, 'Elusive Mistress', p. 498. There may have been assignations with other women on 3 December 1465 and 4 May 1466 (Kleineke, *Edward IV*, p. 79).

20. Waurin, *Anchiennes Cronicques*, pp. 326–7.

21. Kleineke, *Edward IV*, p. 82, citing TNA, C81/848/3926; Joanna L. Chamberlayne, 'A Paper Crown: The Titles and Seals of Cecily, Duchess of York', *The Ricardian*, x, 133 (1996), pp. 430–32; J. L. Laynesmith, 'The Piety of Cecily, Duchess of York', in *The Yorkist Age*, ed. Kleineke and Steer, pp. 35–7.

22. For a recent discussion of the marriage and its impact see Michael Hicks, *Edward V: The Prince in the Tower* (Stroud: Tempus, 2003), pp. 37–51.

23. *The Travels of Leo of Rozmital*, ed. and trans. M. Letts (Hakluyt Society, 2nd series, cviii, 1957), pp. 46–7.

24. Hughes, *Arthurian Myths*, pp. 164–76.

25. Gairdner, *Paston Letters*, IV, p. 275 (Davis, *Paston Letters*, I, p. 396); C. F. Richmond, *The Paston Family in the Fifteenth Century: Endings* (Manchester: Manchester University Press, 2000), pp. 146–8.

26. J. R. Lander, 'Marriage and Politics in the Fifteenth Century', in *Crown and Nobility*, pp. 94–126; Hicks, *Edward IV*, pp. 107–14; idem, 'The Changing Role of the Wydevilles in Yorkist Politics to 1483', in *Patronage, Pedigree and Power*, ed. Charles Ross (Gloucester: Alan Sutton, 1979), pp. 60–73; Andrew Kettle, 'Parvenues in Politics: The Woodvilles, Edward IV and the Baronage, 1464–1469', *The Ricardian*, xiv (2005), pp. 94–12.

27. *Great Chronicle*, p. 208.

28. Ross, *Edward IV*, pp. 104–10, Pollard, *Warwick the Kingmaker*, pp. 59–61.

4. WINTER OF DISCONTENT

1. For these years see Ross, *Edward IV*, pp. 110–25, Pollard, *Warwick the Kingmaker*, pp. 60–65.

2. Warkworth, *Chronicle*, p. 4.

3. Ibid., p. 12.

4. For detailed discussion of the years of crisis see Ross, *Edward IV*, pp. 126–77; shorter accounts are to be found in Kleineke, *Edward IV*, pp. 93–122 and Pollard, *Warwick the Kingmaker*, pp. 65–74.

5. Warkworth, *Chronicle*, p. 9.

6. The events are reported from the crown's perspective in the *Chronicle of the Rebellion in Lincolnshire*, ed. J. G. Nichols (London: Camden, 1847).

7. Commynes, *Memoirs*, pp. 188–9, Anne F. Sutton and Livia Visser-Fuchs, ' "Chevalerie . . . in som partie is worthi forto be comendid, and in some part to ben amendid": Chivalry and the Yorkist Kings', in *St George's Chapel, Windsor, in the Late Middle Ages*, ed. Colin Richmond and Eileen Scarff (Dean and Canons of Windsor, 2001), p. 112.

8. The *Arrivall of Edward IV* gives a first-hand account from within Edward's entourage of his recovery of the throne.

9. *Arrivall of Edward IV*, pp. 13–14.

10. Ibid., p. 20.

11. Warkworth, *Chronicle*, pp. 18–19.

12. Ibid., p. 21. The author of the *Arrivall*, p. 38, would have his readers believe that Henry died of 'pure displeasure and melancholy' on hearing of the collapse of his cause.

5. MASTER OF ALL HIS FOES

1. *Great Chronicle*, pp. 220–21.
2. Warkworth, *Chronicle*, pp. 21–2.
3. *Polydore Vergil's English History*, ed. Ellis, pp. 154–5.
4. Warkworth, *Chronicle*, p. 25; Ross, *Edward IV*, pp. 377–8 for the recoinage, pp. 351–3 for his private trading activities.
5. Ross, *John de Vere*, pp. 69–76.
6. Sutton and Visser-Fuchs, *Royal Funerals*, p. 86.
7. M. A. Hicks, 'Descent, Partition and Extinction: The Warwick Inheritance', *Bulletin of the Institute of Historical Research*, lii (1979), reprinted in Hicks, *Richard III and His Rivals* (London: Hambledon, 1991), pp. 323–36.
8. Gairdner, *Paston Letters*, V, pp. 135–6; Davis, *Paston Letters*, I, no. 277.
9. Gairdner, *Paston Letters*, V, pp. 188–9; Davis, *Paston Letters*, I, no. 281.
10. M. A. Hicks, *False Fleeting Perjur'd Clarence: George, Duke of Clarence, 1449–1478* (Gloucester: Alan Sutton, 1980), pp. 122–3.
11. *Crowland Chronicle Continuations*, pp. 132–3.
12. D. A. L. Morgan, 'The King's Affinity in the Polity of Yorkist England', *TRHS*, 5th series, xxiii (1973); Carpenter, *Wars of the Roses*, pp. 183–96; Hicks, *Edward IV*, pp. 210–22.
13. See Ross, *Edward IV*, pp. 205–26 for the diplomatic, financial and military planning. An alternative view of Edward's intentions is to be found in J. R. Lander, 'The Hundred Years' War and Edward IV's 1475 Campaign in France', in *Crown and Nobility*, pp. 220–41.
14. *Literae Cantuarienses*, ed. J. B. Sheppard (Rolls Series, 1889), III, pp. 284–5.
15. Ibid., pp. 177–9.
16. *Crowland Chronicle Continuations*, pp. 143–5.
17. *Great Chronicle*, p. 223.
18. W. H. St John Hope, *Windsor Castle: An Architectural History* (London: Country Life, 1913), pp. ii, 176.
19. Commynes, *Memoirs*, pp. 238–65 gives a first-hand account of events from the French point of view. For the campaign see Ross, *Edward IV*, pp. 226–34.
20. Commynes, *Memoirs*, pp. 243–59 gives a full eyewitness account of the negotiations.
21. Kingsford, *Chronicles of London*, p. 16; *Calendar of State Papers of Milan, I, 1385–1618*, ed. A. B. Hinds (London: HMSO, 1913), p. 220.
22. Ibid, pp. 238–9.
23. Sutton and Visser-Fuchs, *Royal Funerals*, p. 86; *Crowland Chronicle Continuations*, p. 137.
24. *Crowland Chronicle Continuations*, p. 137; Ross, *Edward IV*, pp. 236–7.

6. THE SUN IN SPLENDOUR

1. Commynes, *Memoirs*, pp. 188, 250.
2. Ross, *Edward IV*, p. 10.

3. Anne F. Sutton and Livia Visser-Fuchs with P. W. Hammond, *The Reburial of Richard Duke of York, 21–30 July 1476* (London: Richard III Society, 1996), passim.

4. *Crowland Chronicle Continuations*, p. 149. For detailed discussion see Ross, *Edward IV*, pp. 299–330, Kleineke, *Edward IV*, pp. 177–97 and for the political dimension D. A. L. Morgan, 'The House of Policy: The Political Role of the Late Plantagenet Household, 1422–1485', in David Starkey et al., *The English Court from the Wars of the Roses to the Civil War* (Harlow: Longman, 1987), pp. 55–70.

5. 'The Records of Bluemantle Pursuivant', in C. L. Kingsford, *English Historical Literature in the Fifteenth Century* (Oxford: Oxford University Press, 1913), pp. 385–8.

6. Mancini, *Usurpation*, p. 65.

7. *Crowland Chronicle Continuations*, p. 149; Ross, *Edward IV*, pp. 261–4.

8. Janet Backhouse, 'Founders of the Royal Library', in *England in the Fifteenth Century*, ed. D. Williams (Woodbridge: Boydell, 1987), pp. 23–30.

9. For the following two paragraphs see Charles Farris, 'The New Edwardians: Royal Piety in the Yorkist Age', in *The Yorkist Age*, ed. Kleineke and Steer, pp. 44–64; Kleineke, *Edward IV*, pp. 182–6.

10. *Crowland Chronicle Continuations*, p. 151.

11. Tim Tatton-Brown, 'The Constructional Sequence and Topography of the Chapel and College Buildings at St George's Chapel', in Richmond and Scarff, *St George's Chapel Windsor*, pp. 3–15.

12. Sutton and Visser-Fuchs, 'Chevalrie', pp. 125–9.

13. Commynes, *Memoirs*, p. 265.

14. Mancini, *Usurpation*, p. 65.

15. Ibid.

16. Commynes, *Memoirs*, pp. 188, 361, 414.

17. *Crowland Chronicle Continuations*, p. 153.

18. Mancini, *Usurpation*, p. 67.

19. Hughes, *Arthurian Myths*, pp. 197–200; T. Lang, 'Medical Recipes from the Yorkist Court', *The Ricardian*, xx (2010), pp. 94–102, especially at pp. 98–9 for plague prevention; *Notes and Queries* (1878), I, p. 343 for the medicine. I owe this reference to Dr Lang.

20. P. W. Hammond, 'The Illegitimate Children of Edward IV', in *Tant d'Emprises – So Many Undertakings: Essays in Honour of Anne F. Sutton*, ed. Livia Visser-Fuchs, *The Ricardian* xiii (2003), pp. 229–33; Kleineke, *Edward IV*, p. 80.

21. More, *History*, p. 5.

22. Ibid.

23. Ibid., p. 73.

24. Mancini, *Usurpation*, pp. 66–7. Armstrong translated *contumeliosus* as 'insolent' rather than the alternative 'abusive'.

25. Ibid. The Greys and Woodvilles were denounced by Richard III as libertines (p. 113, n. 30).

26. *Rot Parl*, V, p. 240; *PROME*, Richard III, Texts/Translations, no. 3.1 [5].

27. Anne F. Sutton and Livia Visser-Fuchs, '"A Most Benevolent Queen": Queen Elizabeth Woodville's Reputation, her Piety and her Books', *The Ricardian*, x (1995), pp. 224–6 and *Royal Funerals*, p. 68; A. J. Pollard, 'Elizabeth Woodville and her Historians', in *Traditions and Transformations in Late Medieval England*, ed. Douglas Biggs et al. (Leiden: Brill, 2002), pp. 145–58; J. L. Laynesmith,

The Last Medieval Queens: English Queenship, 1445–1503 (Oxford: Oxford University Press, 2004), pp. 15–20, 118–19, 173–4, 195–9, 200–25, 230–36.

28. *Crowland Chronicle Continuations*, p. 149.

29. Ross, *Edward IV*, pp. 249–51.

30. M. K. Jones, '1477 – The Expedition that Never Was', *The Ricardian*, xii, 153 (June 2001), pp. 275–92.

31. Hinds, *Calendar of State Papers of Milan*, p. 176.

32. For this and the following paragraphs see Ross, *Edward IV*, pp. 239–45; J. R. Lander, 'The Treason and Death of the Duke of Clarence', in *Crown and Nobility*, pp. 242–66; Hicks, *False Fleeting Perjur'd Clarence*, pp. 128–69 and, for how historians have interpreted it, idem, *Edward IV*, pp. 191–200.

33. *Crowland Chronicle Continuations*, pp. 145–7.

34. But see Hicks, *Edward IV*, pp. 199–200, who offers a spirited apology for 'an able prince . . . neither a fool nor inept'.

35. More, *History*, p. 9.

36. Mancini, *Usurpation*, p. 63.

7. IN FEAR OF NO ONE

1. *Crowland Chronicle Continuations*, p. 147.

2. Ross, *Edward IV*, p. 336.

3. Hicks, *Edward V*, pp. 91–121.

4. A. J. Pollard, *North-Eastern England during the Wars of the Roses* (Oxford: Clarendon Press, 1990), pp. 316–41; R. E. Horrox, *Richard III : A Study of Service* (Cambridge: Cambridge University Press, 1989), pp. 27–88.

5. Ross, *Edward IV*, pp. 248–9, 335–6.

6. *Crowland Chronicle Continuations*, p. 147.

7. C. A. Rawcliffe, *The Stafford Earls of Stafford and Dukes of Buckingham, 1394–1521* (Cambridge: Cambridge University Press, 1978), pp. 28–9.

8. *Crowland Chronicle Continuations*, p. 147.

9. Pollard, *North-Eastern England*, p. 337.

10. Ross, *Edward IV*, pp. 299–307, Hicks, *Edward IV*, pp. 149–52, T. Westerveldt, 'Warrants under the signet in the reign of Edward IV', *Historical Research*, lxxxiii, no. 222 (2010), pp. 602–16.

11. Ross, *Edward IV*, p. 400.

12. Ibid, pp. 318–19.

13. See above, pp. 57, 81.

14. Mancini, *Usurpation*, p. 63; Pollard, *North-Eastern England*, pp. 328–39.

15. See above, pp. 76–8.

16. But see Carpenter, *Wars of the Roses*, pp. 193–6, 205 for a contrary view.

17. Ross, *Edward IV*, pp. 308–12; J. R. Lander, 'The Yorkist Council and Administration' and 'Council, Adminstration and Councillors, 1461–85', in *Crown and Nobility*, pp. 171–90, 191–219.

18. Sir John Fortescue, 'The Governance of England', especially chs 15 and 19, in *The Politics of Fifteenth-Century England*, ed. Kekewich et al., pp. 244–6, 248–9. See also J. L. Watts, ' "A Newe Ffundacion of is Crowne": Monarchy in the Age of Henry VII', in *The Reign of Henry VII*, ed. Benjamin Thompson (Stamford: Paul

Watkins, 1995), pp. 31–53 and Anthony Gross, *The Dissolution of the Lancastrian Kingship: Sir John Fortescue and the Crisis of Monarchy in Fifteenth-Century England* (Stamford: Paul Watkins, 1996), pp. 7–13. For discussion of 'New Monarchy' see Anthony Goodman, *The New Monarchy: England 1471–1534* (Oxford: Basil Blackwell, 1988).

19. Fortescue, 'Governance of England', chs 3–8, pp. 228–35; Watts, 'Newe Ffundacion', p. 42.

20. *Crowland Chronicle Continuations*, pp. 137–9.

21. Ibid., p. 147.

22. S. B. Chrimes, *English Constitutional Ideas of the Fifteenth Century* (Cambridge: Cambridge University Press, 1936), p. 172.

23. B. P. Wolffe, *The Crown Lands, 1461–1536* (London: George Allen and Unwin, 1970), pp. 51–65; Ross, *Edward IV*, pp. 371–87, Hicks, *Edward IV*, pp. 153–64; Carpenter, *Wars of the Roses*, pp. 199–203.

24. Sutton and Visser-Fuchs, *Royal Funerals*, p. 83. 'Mist' can mean either 'I must have their prayers for forgiveness' or 'I didn't listen to their prayers and now ask for forgiveness'.

25. Warkworth, *Chronicle*, pp. 3, 12; Mancini, *Usurpation*, p. 67; *Crowland Chronicle Continuations*, p. 151.

26. *Crowland Chronicle Continuations*, p. 153.

27. 'Financial Memoranda of the Reign of Edward V', ed. R. E. Horrox, in *Camden Miscellany*, xxix (London: Camden 4th series, XXXIV, 1987), pp. 209–12.

28. A. J. Pollard, *Late Medieval England, 1399–1509* (Harlow: Longman, 2000), pp. 310–11.

29. Commynes, *Memoirs*, p. 394.

30. For recent discussions of foreign policy in the last five years of the reign see Ross, *Edward IV*, pp. 251–6, 278–95; Kleineke, *Edward IV*, pp. 147–53; Pollard, *North-Eastern England*, pp. 233–41; Jelle Haemers and Frederik Buylaert, 'War, Politics and Diplomacy in England, France and the Low Countries, 1475–1500', in *The Yorkist Age*, ed. Kleineke and Steer, pp. 201–13.

31. *Crowland Chronicle Continuations*, p. 151.

8. THE END OF SUMMER

1. *Crowland Chronicle Continuations*, p. 149.

2. Ross, *Edward IV*, pp. 292–5; Pollard, *North-Eastern England*, pp. 239–40.

3. Ross, *Edward IV*, pp. 336–7.

4. Mancini, *Usurpation*, p. 67; More, *History*, p. 5; Commynes, *Memoirs*, p. 414. The Crowland chronicler also described him as gross (*Crowland Chronicle Continuations*, p. 153).

5. *Great Chronicle*, p. 228; More, *History*, p. 6 has Windsor. *Crowland Chronicle Continuations*, p. 149.

6. Ross, *Edward IV*, pp. 414–15 discusses the contemporary speculation.

7. *Crowland Chronicle Continuations*, p. 153; *Excerpta Historica*, ed. S. Bentley (London: Samuel Bentley, 1831), pp. 366–79.

8. Mancini, *Usurpation*, p. 69, elaborated by More, *History*, p. 11.

9. *Crowland Chronicle Continuations*, pp. 151–3.

10. Sutton and Visser-Fuchs, *Royal Funerals*, pp. 7–14.
11. Ibid., pp. 14–31.
12. Ibid., pp. 93–110.
13. Ibid., pp. 75–92.
14. Many accounts exist of these events and the fate of Edward IV's sons. See in particular Charles Ross, *Richard III* (New Haven and London: Yale University Press, 1999), pp. 63–104; Horrox, *Richard III*, pp. 89–137; Hicks, *Edward V*, pp. 137–93; and for the sons A. J. Pollard, *Richard III and the Princes in the Tower* (Stroud: Alan Sutton, 1991), pp. 115–43.
15. Summarized in Pollard, *Richard III and the Princes*, pp. 90–106 and more recently David Hipshon, *Richard III* (Abingdon: Routledge, 2011), pp. 119–36.
16. *Ecclesiastes* 10:16.
17. Reiterated most recently in Carpenter, *Wars of the Roses*, pp. 208–10.
18. Richmond, '1465 and All That', pp. 186–95.
19. *Crowland Chronicle Continuations*, p. 133.
20. Jones, *Bosworth*, pp. 58–63, 73–8, 82. But see Laynesmith, 'The Piety of Cecily, Duchess of York', p. 35, and Christopher Harper Bill, *ODNB*, X, p. 798, who cast her in the role of family mediator.
21. Watts, 'Newe Ffundacion', pp. 49–50.

Further Reading

GENERAL WORKS

The standard modern account of Edward IV's reign is Charles Ross, *Edward IV* (London: Eyre Methuen, 1974). The most detailed narrative, drawing exhaustively on record sources but somewhat dated in interpretation, is Cora Scofield, *The Life and Reign of Edward the Fourth*, 2 vols (London: Longmans, Green & Co., 1923). An excellent, shorter account is Hannes Kleineke, *Edward IV* (Abingdon: Routledge, 2009). A. J. Pollard, *Late Medieval England, 1300–1509* (Harlow: Longman, 2000), pp. 268–323, contains an earlier consideration of the reign, differing in some detail and emphasis from this work. Jonathan Hughes, *Arthurian Myths and Alchemy: The Kingship of Edward IV* (Stroud: Sutton, 2002) seeks to uncover a complex personality shaped by contemporary superstition and intellectual traditions.

There are several introductory works on the broader context of the Wars of the Roses, including M. C. Carpenter, *The Wars of the Roses: Politics and the Constitution in England, c.1437–1509* (Cambridge: Cambridge University Press, 1997); Anthony Goodman, *The Wars of the Roses: Military Activity and English Society, 1452–97* (London: Routledge & Kegan Paul, 1981); David Grummitt, *The Wars of the Roses* (London: I. B. Taurus, 2013); Michael Hicks, *The Wars of the Roses* (New Haven and London: Yale University Press, 2010); A. J. Pollard, *The Wars of the Roses* (Basingstoke: Macmillan Palgrave, 3rd edn 2012); Charles Ross, *The Wars of the Roses* (London: Thames and Hudson, 1976).

Articles on Edward IV and his reign are to be found in *The Ricardian*, the journal of the Richard III Society, and the annually published *Fifteenth Century* edited by Linda Clark. Several of these are cited in the endnotes.

SOURCES

The best modern introduction to the narrative sources is provided by Antonia Gransden, *Historical Writing in England: II, c.1307 to the Early Sixteenth Century* (London: Routledge & Kegan Paul, 1982). Michael Hicks provides a useful discussion of record evidence in 'The Sources', in A. J. Pollard (ed.), *The Wars of the Roses*, 1996 (Basingstoke: Macmillan, 1995), pp. 20–40. Selections are to be found in J. R. Lander, *The Wars of the Roses* (New York: Capricorn Books, 1967) and Keith Dockray, *Edward IV: A Sourcebook* (Stroud: Sutton, 1999). Michael Hicks, *Edward IV* (London: Arnold, Hodder Education, 2004) discusses the sources and historiography for the reign; see in particular pp. 40–53 on the 'rival assessments' of the Crowland Continuator and Commynes. For More see the introduction by R. S. Sylvester to his edition *The History of Richard III* in the complete works of St Thomas More published by Yale University Press, vol. 2 (New Haven, 1963). Alison Hanham, *Richard III and His Early Historians* (Oxford: Oxford University Press, 1975) considers all the early sources for Richard's reign but has much to say that is germane to Edward IV.

POLITICS, GOVERNMENT AND WAR

For biographies of the major players see the *Oxford Dictionary of National Biography*. There are two recent studies of the career of Warwick the Kingmaker: Michael Hicks, *Warwick the Kingmaker*

(Oxford: Blackwell, 1998) and A. J. Pollard, *Warwick the King-maker: Politics, Power and Fame* (London: Hambledon Continuum, 2007). Queen Elizabeth Woodville has yet to receive a modern biography; much can be gleaned however from J. L. Laynesmith, *The Last Medieval Queens: English Queenship, 1445–1503* (Oxford: Oxford University Press, 2004). Discussion of the role of the queen's family is to be found in J. R. Lander, 'Marriage and Politics in the Fifteenth Century: the Nevilles and the Woodvilles', reprinted in *Crown and Nobility, 1450–1509* (London: Edward Arnold, 1976) pp. 94–126 and M. A. Hicks, 'The Changing Role of the Wydevilles in Yorkist Politics to 1483', in *Patronage, Pedigree and Power*, ed. Charles Ross (Gloucester: Alan Sutton, 1979). M. A. Hicks, *False Fleeting Perjur'd Clarence: George, Duke of Clarence, 1449–1478* (Gloucester: Alan Sutton, 1980) remains the best study of the king's mercurial brother. Of the many works on Richard III, Charles Ross, *Richard III* (London: Eyre Methuen, 1974); Rosemary Horrox, *Richard III: A Study of Service* (Cambridge: Cambridge University Press, 1989); and David Hipshon, *Richard III* (Abingdon: Routledge, 2011) deal fully with his career before 1483.

Regional politics can be followed in A. J. Pollard, *North-Eastern England during the Wars of the Roses* (Oxford: Clarendon Press, 1991); M. C. Carpenter, *Locality and Politics: A Study of Warwickshire Landed Society, 1401–1499* (Cambridge: Cambridge University Press, 1992). East Anglian politics can be explored through Helen Castor, *Blood and Roses: The Paston Family in the Fifteenth Century* (London: Faber and Faber, 2004) and more comprehensively in Colin Richmond, *The Paston Family in the Fifteenth Century*, 3 vols (Cambridge and Manchester: Cambridge University Press and Manchester University Press, 1990–2000). An important overview is to be found in D. A. L. Morgan, 'The King's Affinity in the Polity of Yorkist England', *TRHS*, 5th series, 23 (1973). Malcolm Mercer, *The Medieval Gentry: Power, Leadership and Choice during the Wars of the Roses* (London: Continuum, 2010) is a thoughtful examination of the leaders of county societies. For Wales see G. Williams, *Recovery, Reorientation and Reformation, c.1315–1642* (Oxford: Oxford University Press, 1987), pp. 185–242 and Michael Hicks, *Edward V: The Prince in the Tower* (Stroud: Tempus, 2003), pp. 91–122.

A good starting point for Edward IV's government is B. P. Wolffe, *Yorkist and Early Tudor Government, 1461–1509* (London: Historical Association, 1966). A broader perspective is taken in Anthony Goodman, *The New Monarchy: England, 1471–1534* (Oxford: Basil Blackwell, 1988). J. L. Watts, *The Making of Politics: Europe 1300–1500* (Cambridge: Cambridge University Press, 2009) puts English developments in a wider context. Edward IV's Chamber finance can be approached through B. P. Wolffe, *The Royal Demesne in English History* (London: George Allen and Unwin, 1971). The council and councillors are explored in J. R. Lander, 'The Yorkist Council' and 'Council, Administration and Councillors, 1461–85', both reprinted in *Crown and Nobility*, pp. 171–90, 191–219. Kleineke's *Edward IV*, pp. 164–76, is an excellent introduction to parliament and taxation during the reign.

David Santiuste, *Edward IV and the Wars of the Roses* (Barnsley: Pen and Sword, 2010) contains the best discussion of Edward's career as a soldier from 1461 to 1471. His battles are refought and won in several works, most revealingly Towton and Barnet in Glenn Foard and Richard K. Morris, *Fields of Conflict* (York: Council for British Archaeology, 2011), Towton in Tim Sutherland, 'Killing Time: Challenging Perceptions of Three Medieval Conflicts – Ferrybridge, Dintingdale and Towton', *Journal of Battlefield Archaeology*, v (2009) and John Saddler, *Towton: The Battle of Palm Sunday* (Barnsley: Pen and Sword, 2011); and the victories of 1471 in P. W. Hammond, *The Battles of Barnet and Tewkesbury* (Gloucester: Alan Sutton, 1990).

For Edward's court and private life see Ross, *Edward IV*, chapter 11; D. A. L. Morgan, 'The House of Policy', in David Starkey et al., *The English Court from the Wars of the Roses to the Civil War*

(Harlow: Longman, 1987), pp. 55–70; Anne F. Sutton and Livia Visser-Fuchs, 'Chivalry and the Yorkist Kings', in *St George's Chapel, Windsor, in the Late Middle Ages*, ed. Colin Richmond and Eileen Scarff (Windsor: Dean and Canons of Windsor, 2001), pp. 109–31; Charles Farris, 'The New Edwardians: Royal Piety in the Yorkist Age', in *The Yorkist Age*, ed. Hannes Kleineke and Christian Steer (Donington: Shaun Tyas, 2013), pp. 44–63.

Picture Credits

1. Wheel of fortune (© 2016 The British Library Board, BL Royal 18 D II, fol. 6)
2. Jousting (© 2016 The British Library Board, Cotton Julius E. IV, art. 6)
3. Edward IV witnessing the execution of the Duke of Somerset (Ghent University Library)
4. Elizabeth Woodville and daughters. Stained glass at Little Malvern Priory (Little Malvern, Worcestershire/ Bridgeman Images)
5. Garter stall plate for William, Lord Hastings, St George's Windsor (The Dean and Canons of Windsor)
6. Earl Rivers presents 'The Dictes and Sayings of the Philosophers' to Edward IV and family (Lambeth Palace Library, MS 265, fol. VI)
7. Portrait of Edward IV *c.*1520, based on an original *c.*1470–75 (Royal Collection Trust © Her Majesty Queen Elizabeth II, 2016/Bridgeman Images)
8. Wing of tabernacle with head of St John the Baptist with white rose and sun in splendour (© CSG CIC Glasgow Museums and Libraries Collections)
9. Gates to the intended site of Edward IV's tomb, St George's Windsor (The Dean and Canons of Windsor)

Index

Penguin Monarchs

THE HOUSES OF WESSEX AND DENMARK

THE HOUSES OF NORMANDY, BLOIS AND ANJOU

THE HOUSE OF PLANTAGENET

THE HOUSES OF LANCASTER AND YORK

* Now in paperback

THE HOUSE OF TUDOR

Henry VII   Sean Cunningham
Henry VIII*   John Guy
Edward VI*   Stephen Alford
Mary I*   John Edwards
Elizabeth I*   Helen Castor

THE HOUSE OF STUART

James I*   Thomas Cogswell
Charles I*   Mark Kishlansky
[Cromwell*   David Horspool]
Charles II*   Clare Jackson
James II*   David Womersley
William III & Mary II*   Jonathan Keates
Anne   Richard Hewlings

THE HOUSE OF HANOVER

George I*   Tim Blanning
George II   Norman Davies
George III   Amanda Foreman
George IV   Stella Tillyard
William IV*   Roger Knight
Victoria*   Jane Ridley

THE HOUSES OF SAXE-COBURG & GOTHA AND WINDSOR

Edward VII*   Richard Davenport-Hines
George V*   David Cannadine
Edward VIII*   Piers Brendon
George VI*   Philip Ziegler
Elizabeth II*   Douglas Hurd

* Now in paperback